Duncan Hines

Cake Mix Magic

Have Fun
Mixing up Some Magic ☆
Happy Birthday
xox
Beth, Jeff,
Sam, Rebecca

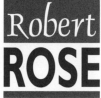

Robert
ROSE

Cake Mix Magic

For complete cataloguing information, see page 4.

DESIGN, EDITORIAL AND PRODUCTION:	MATTHEWS COMMUNICATIONS DESIGN INC.
PHOTOGRAPHY:	MARK T. SHAPIRO
ART DIRECTION/FOOD PHOTOGRAPHY:	SHARON MATTHEWS
FOOD STYLIST:	KATE BUSH
PROP STYLIST:	CHARLENE ERRICSON
MANAGING EDITOR:	PETER MATTHEWS
COPY EDITOR:	KIRSTEN HANSON
INDEXER:	BARBARA SCHON
COLOR SCANS:	POINTONE GRAPHICS

Cover photo: piece of CRUNCH 'N' CREAM CHOCOLATE TORTE *(page 39)*

We acknowledge the financial support of the Government of Canada through the Book Publishing Industry Development Program (BPIDP) for our publishing activities.

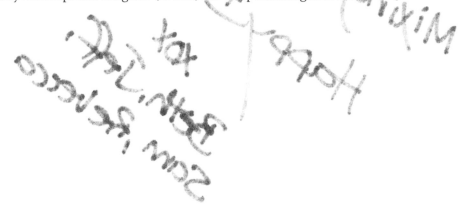

Published by: Robert Rose Inc. • 120 Eglinton Ave. E, Suite 1000, Toronto, Ontario, Canada M4P 1E2 Tel: (416) 322-6552

Printed in Canada

1234567 BP 04 03 02 01

CONTENTS

National Library of Canada Cataloguing in Publication Data

Snider, Jill, 1947–
    Cake mix magic

Includes index.
ISBN 0-7788-0029-6

1. Baking.   2. Food mixes.   I. Title.

TX763.S64 2001   641.8'15   C2001-930006-9

ACKNOWLEDGMENTS

I'd like to express my sincere thanks to the many people who helped to make this book a reality. A book is very much a team effort and without them I couldn't have done it.

My publisher, Bob Dees, for his patience, understanding, encouragement and guidance on the numerous occasions I was ready to quit when I was sure I could never meet his expectations.

Danielle Szostak for her endless support and encouragement on the cake mix project, without which I couldn't have done the book. Also to Danielle and her family, who tasted cake after cake after cake, giving me valuable, detailed feedback on each one.

Brenda Venedam, who diligently typed recipe copy until I'm sure her fingers couldn't type any longer, and who, with her family, cheerfully tasted many many cakes, giving honest feedback on every one.

My mother, Teddy, who never questioned my crazy working hours and was always willing to give me her honest opinion on just one more cake. Also for her influence, which made me appreciate and love everything "home baked" and want to carry on her tradition.

To Robin Hood, who let me test many of the recipes in their test kitchen and recruit the staff for tasters. Thanks to their critical evaluation, and letting me "test 'til perfect", I think we've ended up with the best cake mix recipes possible.

INTRODUCTION

Cake in some form plays an important role in the lives of most people, whether it is a simple morning coffee cake, a treat with afternoon tea, a lunch-box sweet, an anytime snack or an after-dinner dessert. And of course, birthdays without a cake will never happen. Cake can be as plain and simple or as elegant and decadent as the occasion calls for.

As the hours of free time available for baking decrease in today's hectic world, a baker's need for shortcuts that don't sacrifice quality increases. Anyone who bakes from scratch knows that cake baking not only can be time-consuming, but it can also end up in disappointing results. I love to bake from scratch but if there is a convenience food that saves me time and still meets my high standards for quality, I'm happy to use it as part of my baking. I call it speedy scratch baking! Starting with a Duncan Hines® cake mix is the perfect shortcut you're looking for. You're off to a good start when you start with the best. Since the cake mix ingredients are premeasured accurately and are consistently reliable, starting with a mix saves many preparation steps like measuring, sifting and creaming. A cake mix also cuts down considerably on the number of ingredients you need to create a dazzling dessert. You can still add some of the wonderful rich, flavorful ingredients like eggs, sour cream, butter, nuts, chocolate and fruits that give the cake that "homemade" distinction and taste that no bakery cake can match.

The tolerance of cake mixes is another bonus, greatly reducing the risk of a disaster dessert. Mixes are formulated to withstand minor variations such as overmixing, undermixing, oven temperature variations, measuring utensil discrepancies, different mixers and pans and a variety of added ingredients. You are almost guaranteed to be proud of your masterpiece. And if by chance you aren't, my solution is always the same: Don't apologize, just serve your cake warm with a big scoop of vanilla ice cream. Everyone will be happy and none the wiser!

Having a cake mix and a few other ingredients on hand rules out the excuse that you don't have time to bake cakes. It's a great way to be prepared for the unexpected.

In this book I've tried to include a selection of cakes that will carry you through every occasion. The recipes are easy to follow, using common ingredients that you'll have on hand or that are readily available at your local grocery store. Each chapter offers a wide variety of flavors and ingredients, and I've made suggestions for variations on the cakes and frostings to suit different tastes. I'm sure you'll think of more combinations as well. With a little imagination and creativity, the possibilities are endless.

Single-layer cakes are usually quick and easy to prepare. They are often glazed or frosted right in the pan – an ideal choice for casual entertaining, bake sales, pot luck and lunch boxes. Upside-down cakes also fall into this category. They range from the classic Pineapple to more exotic Bumbleberry.

Multi-layer cakes take more time to complete, as the layers are filled, frosted and decorated. However, the cake portion is often very simple to make. Results are well worth the extra time and effort. These lovely creations are wonderful for the special occasions when you want to impress your guests.

Bundt cakes and tube cakes include a combination of everyday and special. They are generally quick and easy to make. They lend themselves to the addition of other ingredients like nuts, puréed vegetables, fruits, etc. Their shape is always impressive. Finish these with a simple glaze, a dusting of confectioner's sugar or a frosting.

Coffee cakes are always a favorite. As the name implies, they are a perfect match for a cup of steaming coffee, cappuccino or tea at anytime of the day. They aren't too sweet and often contain fresh fruit

Loaves and muffins are another favorite coffee accompaniment. These recipes usually freeze well. You can't go wrong with an extra Cranberry Banana Loaf in the freezer.

For **special occasion cakes** you will spend a little more time, but they are made easier with a cake mix beginning. You can even make **cheesecakes** – a perfect choice to serve to guests – using a cake mix to start. I also offer some recipes for holiday treats using traditional flavors you make once or twice a year like pumpkin and candied fruit. However, don't feel you have to limit the Pumpkin Cake to Thanksgiving. It's fabulous any time.

I've included a chapter called "**Desserts**", which offers recipes that start with a mix but aren't really cakes. Comfort food cobblers and crumbles are made easy. You'll also find chilly desserts like trifle, mousse cakes and many make-ahead dishes here.

The versatility of the cake mix takes it far beyond the cake category. I actually amazed myself and was delighted with the recipes for **cookies**, as well as **bars** and **squares**. Because many of the recipes were adapted from my favorite scratch recipes to include the use of a cake mix, I find it very hard to pick a favorite. But that's not a problem, since a selection of bars and cookies make up a wonderful cookie tray.

This book wouldn't be complete without frostings and fillings to finish these masterpieces. There's one here to suit every cake so you can mix, match and choose your favorites.

Among this wide array of recipes I'm sure you'll find a few that will become your favorites to eat as well as to make. There really is something here for every taste! Treat the recipes as a beginning, adding your own personal touches, and most of all – *enjoy cake mix baking!*

Baking Equipment

PANS

Today's baking pans are not as standardized as they once were. They differ in size and shape from older ones and they also vary from one manufacturer to another. The labeling consists of an often-confusing mixture of imperial and metric measurements. Although I recommend using the pan size specified in the recipes, you can substitute a pan that is similar in dimension and volume. Don't use pans smaller in volume (the cake may overflow); slightly larger is usually safe, although the cake will be shallower and require less baking time. You can interchange shapes (e.g. round instead of square) if the volume is the same and it is not much deeper, shallower, longer or shorter. Measurements are done on the inside across the top of the pan. To confirm the volume of a pan, fill it with water and pour into a measuring cup.

You will need these common pans to prepare cakes in this book:

- A 13- by 9-inch (3.5 L) pan
- Two or three 8-inch (1.2 L) round pans
- Two or three 9-inch (1.5 L) round pans
- A 10-inch (3 L) bundt pan
- A 10-inch (4 L) tube pan
- An 8- to 10-inch (2 to 3 L) springform pan
- Two 8- by 4-inch (1.5 L) or 9- by 5-inch (2 L) loaf pans
- Two muffin (cupcake) pans (12 cups each)
- A 17- by 11-inch (3 L) jelly roll pan
- Baking sheets

I prefer good quality, shiny metal pans for baking. They bake evenly and don't rust. If you use glass, remember to decrease the temperature by 25° F (10° C). If using nonstick pans, follow manufacturer's directions. Most recommend decreasing the temperature by 25° F (10° C) since nonstick surfaces, especially dark ones, bake faster. This adjustment is especially important for large cakes because the edges will overbake before the center is done.

MIXER

Use an electric countertop mixer or a good-quality hand mixer, not the heavy-duty commercial type which are too powerful for normal consumer-style baking. If you do a lot of baking, the countertop model is much more efficient and easier to use.

BOWLS

I prefer metal or glass. Plastic does not work well for beaten egg whites. Have a few of each size – small, medium and large. Most of the batters in this book are prepared in a large mixer bowl. I refer to the bowl needed for electric mixer as a "mixer" bowl. If this isn't specified, other bowls will do (for example, when mixing a crumble topping, or fruit with sugar).

RACKS

Wire racks are essential for cooling cakes. Choose stainless steel, since they won't rust and have a long life. It's a good idea to have a variety of sizes (round, square, rectangle) to suit the size of cakes you are making. Look for racks that have narrow spaces between the steel wires. I also keep one rack covered with a thick tea towel pinned securely in place. Turn cakes out onto this and you won't get rack marks on top of your cake. When necessary, remove and wash towel!

KNIVES

A long, sharp serrated knife with a blade about 12 inches (30 cm) long makes cutting cakes horizontally a breeze. However, some people prefer to use dental floss for an even slice. Try both methods and pick your favorite. Electric knives are excellent for angel food cakes.

Know Your Ingredients

1. CAKE MIXES

Cake mixes contain many of the same ingredients you'd require for baking cakes from scratch. They are already premeasured in the correct proportion. These include flour, sugar, leavening (baking powder and baking soda), fat, salt, flavoring and coloring. For a standard cake-mix cake, you have to add eggs, oil and water. Cake mixes will also contain other ingredients not found in your kitchen cupboard, such as emulsifiers, conditioners and thickeners; these are added to make the mix, more tolerant so they'll perform well no matter what a consumer might do to them! A little more or less water, large or small eggs, more or less oil, underbeating, overbeating – all of these can be tolerated. Of course, they do perform best when the recommended measurements and method are followed!

Cake mixes also provide the benefit of a one-year shelf life when stored unopened in a cool dry place. This makes it very convenient to add it to your list of "staple ingredients" so it's on hand whenever you need it. I like to have 2 white, 2 chocolate, 2 lemon, 1 spice and 1 marble cake mix always on my shelf. With these you are ready to make just about any recipe in the book. I personally prefer white over yellow cake, since the flavor is not as strong and is therefore more versatile. In many recipes they are interchangeable. You should compare the two in a few recipes and pick your favorite. Flavors also vary considerably with manufacturer. You'll also find several flavors of chocolate mixes are available. Again, use your favorite.

Every recipe has been tested using Duncan Hines® cake mixes. When you start with a supreme quality product you're likely to end up with a dessert you'll be proud of.

2. FATS

It's important to use the type of fat recommended in the recipe. This is what has been used in testing. Sometimes a liquid (oil, melted butter) is used and sometimes a solid fat (butter) is required.

Vegetable oil. This is the most common fat required in cake mix recipes. It works well with the mix ingredients to give you a light, tender, moist cake. Select a light, flavorless oil such as canola, safflower, sunflower or corn rather than heavier varieties such as olive oil.

Butter and margarine. I prefer to use lightly salted butter in baking. It has a wonderful flavor and good browning qualities. In most cases hard margarine can be substituted but avoid the soft tub-type margarines or spreads. Hard margarines work well where there are other strong flavors, such as spices and chocolate, and where a "buttery" taste isn't as important.

Shortening. Think of shortening as a solid form of vegetable oil. I use it mainly for greasing the pans rather than as an ingredient. (Cooking sprays are also good for greasing pans.) Oil or butter tend to stick and burn more easily.

3. SUGARS

Granulated sugar (white). I use regular granulated sugar in recipe testing. It is free-flowing and doesn't require sifting. You can also buy superfine or fruit sugar, but I only use this in shortbreads.

Confectioner's sugar. Also referred to as icing sugar, powdered sugar or 10x sugar, this type has been ground to a fine powder. It has approximately 3% cornstarch added to prevent lumping and crystallization in storage. (Be sure to keep the bag airtight.) Confectioner's sugar is used primarily in frostings and glazes. It dissolves almost instantly in liquids, which makes it wonderful for sweetening whipping cream. I prefer to measure it and then sift it. I have based my recipes on this method rather than the reverse, sifting and then measuring.

Brown sugar. This is less refined than granulated sugar. The darker the color, the more molasses and moisture it contains, and hence the stronger the flavor. I like the golden (sometimes called yellow) variety for recipe testing, but light and dark are interchangeable. Brown sugar is used mainly for toppings, streusels and some frostings. It isn't used much in cake batters, since it makes them heavier and too moist. (Cake mixes usually contain sufficient sugar anyway.) However, brown sugar is wonderful for use in cookies and bars which benefit from the denser texture and caramel flavor. To measure, pack it firmly into a dry measuring cup and level off. Because of its moisture, brown sugar tends to lump. Store it airtight in a covered jar or heavy plastic bag in a cool dry place. If it does harden, put it in a plastic bag with a slice of apple for a few days.

4. EGGS

I use "large" eggs for all recipe testing. Remove them from the refrigerator at least 1 hour before using to come to room temperature. If they are to be separated, do this when they are cold, then leave them for the hour. (This will help ensure maximum volume from the whites.) Cover with plastic wrap to prevent drying.

Eggs contribute to leavening, texture, color, flavor, volume, richness and nutritional value in cakes. In other words, they are one of the most important ingredients!

5. LIQUIDS

Water is the most common liquid ingredient used in cake mixes. You'll find it is also used in many of these recipes.

Milk. I use 2% milk as it is the preferred household product. Whole milk (homogenized), low-fat (1%) and non-fat (skim) will also work, although results will vary slightly because of the different fat content.

Buttermilk. This is made from low-fat milk and a bacterial culture. You can find buttermilk in the dairy case of your supermarket, or make up your own. For 1 cup (250 mL) buttermilk, mix 1 tbsp (15 mL) vinegar or lemon juice and enough milk to make 1 cup (250 mL); let stand 5 minutes, then stir.

Evaporated milk. This canned product is made by evaporating milk to half its volume.

It has a mild caramel taste and comes in whole or low-fat versions.

Light cream. This has 10% M.F. (milk fat content), and is also called half-and-half cream.

Table cream. This has 18% M.F. It can be used in recipes calling for light cream.

Whipping cream. This has 35% M.F. and is also called heavy cream.

Sour cream. Regular sour cream is about 14% M.F.; it's also available in low-fat and no-fat versions. Use regular or low-fat in baking. (I don't recommend the no-fat variety). In most recipes plain yogurt can be substituted.

Yogurt. This is available in plain and flavored varieties, with a range of fat contents. As with sour cream, don't use the no-fat type for baking.

Sweetened condensed milk. This is evaporated milk which has been reduced further and sweetened. It is available in whole and low-fat versions. All testing was done using the whole (or regular) version.

6. NUTS

Store nuts in the freezer to keep them fresh. When ready to use, let them thaw and use as directed –, or, for optimum flavor, toast them: Spread nuts out in a single layer on a cookie sheet. Bake at 350° F (180° C) for 5 to 10 minutes, stirring often, until golden and fragrant. Chopped nuts will take less time to toast than whole nuts. For hazelnuts, rub off skins in a tea towel while warm. The weight equivalent of 1 cup (250 mL) lightly toasted nuts is approximately 100 g.

7. COCONUT

Store coconut in freezer as well. Like nuts, coconut has a nicer flavor when toasted. I prefer flaked or shredded coconut in baking. Sweetened or unsweetened is a matter of choice. Toast at 350° F (180° C) about 5 minutes, stirring often. Watch carefully, since it burns quickly.

8. CHOCOLATE

A "must have" ingredient you should never be without! Keep a supply of *semi-sweet* or *bittersweet squares* for chopping, grating or melting in recipes. *Unsweetened chocolate* is not used as often in this book, but keep a small amount on hand for some of the frostings. *Chocolate chips* are formulated to soften but still hold their shape during baking. In general, they are used in and on top of cakes, while squares are used for melting. *White chocolate* is not really chocolate but has come to be a popular ingredient in baking. Be sure to buy pure white chocolate – not artificial, which won't melt properly. *Cocoa* is a dry, unsweetened powder made from chocolate liquor with most of the cocoa butter removed. Cocoa tends to clump in storage, so measure then sift before using.

To Melt Chocolate: Coarsely chop chocolate into pieces. Melt slowly in a double boiler or a bowl set over hot (not boiling) water or microwave on Medium until almost melted. Stir to finish melting completely. You can also melt chocolate in a small saucepan over low heat, stirring constantly until smooth. For chocolate curls, heat a chocolate square in the microwave for 10 seconds just to warm but not melt. Shave warm chocolate with a vegetable peeler to make curls.

9. FLAVORINGS
Always use pure extracts, not artificial. The price is considerably more but well worth it.

10. SPICES
Keep your favorites on hand. Buy in small amounts and store in tightly sealed glass containers in a cool, dark place. Replace within 6 to 9 months.

11. CREAM CHEESE
I prefer full-fat cream cheese but you can substitute a lower-fat version if you wish. For smooth blending use blocks of cream cheese that have been softened to room temperature. Don't use tubs of soft, spreadable cheese.

12. DRIED FRUIT
Keep raisins, apricots, cranberries and dates on hand for general baking, and buy specialty items, such as candied fruit, for holiday baking or as needed. Fruits may sink if a batter is not stiff enough. Chopping fruits finely and

tossing in flour to coat will help to suspend them.

13. FRESH FRUIT
Lemons. One medium lemon yields about 1/4 cup (50 mL) juice and 2 tsp (10 mL) grated zest.

Oranges. Two or three medium oranges yield 1 cup (250 mL) juice and 3 tbsp (45 mL) grated zest.

Apples. One pound (500 g) or 3 medium apples yield about 3 cups (750 mL) sliced or diced.

Bananas. One pound (500 g) or 2 or 3 large bananas yield 1 cup (250 mL) mashed.

Strawberries and raspberries. One pound (500 g) contains about 4 cups (1 L) whole berries, 3 cups (750 mL) sliced or 2 cups (500 mL) crushed.

14. CANNED FRUIT
Keep a supply of the common types like pineapple, (crushed and rings), apricots, peaches and mandarins. Brands will vary in proportion of liquid to solid fruit, as well as in the size of fruit pieces.

15. FROZEN FRUIT
Keep a few bags of cranberries in your freezer, since they can be hard to find in the summer. Buy other frozen fruits, such as rhubarb and berries, as needed.

Cake Baking Tips and Techniques

Before you start. Read the recipe carefully, checking the ingredients, utensils and equipment required, oven temperature and baking time before you start to bake.

Assemble all ingredients and equipment required. It also helps to perform tasks such as chopping or toasting nuts, preparing fruit, or grating zest a head of time, so that mixing is quick and easy.

Have ingredients at room temperature for easy blending. If eggs are to be separated, separate them cold then leave about 1 hour.

Adjust oven rack to middle level for most cake baking. Angel food cakes are baked on the lower rack. Always check cake mix package or recipe for specified directions.

Use the pan size recommended in your recipe.

Prepare pans as required. Grease lightly with shortening or a vegetable cooking spray. Don't use butter, margarine or oil, which are more likely to stick and burn. If pan requires flouring as well, sprinkle greased surface lightly with flour. Shake pan to evenly distribute flour and then shake out excess. Layer cake pans can also be lined with a circle of parchment paper on the bottom for foolproof cake removal. Angel food cakes are an exception. The pan is left ungreased so the batter crawls up, sticking to the sides as it rises during baking. For muffins and cupcakes, paper liners can replace greasing.

Measuring. Accuracy is important. Use liquid (usually glass) measures for liquids. Read the measurement at eye level. For dry ingredients, use dry measuring cups. Spoon ingredients into cup lightly and level off with a straight spatula or knife. Don't tap or pack! For brown sugar however, pack into cup firmly, then level off. It should hold the cup shape when turned out. Measure dry ingredients before sifting and butter before melting unless specified otherwise. Use measuring spoons for small amounts of both liquid and dry ingredients.

Mixing. Mix batters in a large mixer bowl using an electric mixer. Start on low speed for about 30 seconds, just to blend liquid and dry ingredients, and prevent splattering, then increase speed to medium and beat for 2 minutes or until smooth. Scrape bowl often during mixing. For plain cakes, once you spread the batter in the pan, bang the pan firmly against the counter top to eliminate any large air bubbles. Don't do this with angel food cakes, marble cakes or cakes with a streusel or a lot of fruit or nuts throughout.

Baking. Bake cake as soon as it is mixed. The leavening in a mix will start to work as soon as it is moistened. A delay in baking after mixing will result in poor volume. For proper heat distribution pans should not touch each other or the sides of the oven during baking.

Timing. Use recommended baking times as a guideline. Always set timer for 5 minutes before the minimum time given to allow for oven variances. Ovens are often hotter than the temperature indicates and cakes can easily be overdone, especially those high in sugar or baked in a dark pan. It's much safer to add more time in 5-minute segments if cake isn't done.

Testing for doneness. When cakes are done, a toothpick, a wooden skewer or a cake tester inserted in center of cake will come out clean (This test won't work for some cakes with "gooey" ingredients, however.). Another indication is that the top will spring back when lightly touched and it will come away from sides of the pan. For lighter cakes, the color is also a good indicator – it should be a nice golden brown.

Removing cake from the pan. Unless specified otherwise in recipe, allow layer cakes to cool for 10 minutes and 20 minutes for deeper cakes, such as tube cakes and loaves. Leave cake in pan on a wire rack then turn out and cool completely on rack. To remove cake from pan, run knife around edge and center of tube pans then invert, shaking gently to remove cake. Bundt cakes are cooled initially in the pan, then turned out of pan and left to finish cooling fluted side up. All other cakes are inverted twice so they finish cooling in the same position (top side up) as they are baked. Angel food cakes are an exception. The baked cake is immediately turned upside down on a funnel, bottle or glass bottom and left until completely cool.

Glazing and frosting. Glazes are often put on while cakes are warm, while butter icings and creams are put on cakes after they are completely cooled. Often there is no right or wrong frosting or glaze for a cake. It really is a matter of personal preference. Keep in mind both color and flavor when deciding how to finish your cake. I've given several ideas for cake and frosting combinations in most recipes but use this only as a guideline. Duncan Hines® offers an array of ready-to-serve frostings which are an excellent alternative to homemade.

TIPS FOR SIMPLE FROSTING OF LAYER CAKES

Brush off loose crumbs from sides of cake.

Freeze cakes for about 30 minutes. This makes them less fragile and easier to frost.

Put a bit of frosting on the plate. This will hold the cake in place.

If layers are domed you can slice a bit off the top to even them off.

To keep plate clean, set 4 strips of waxed paper, forming a square, under cake edge.

Place first cake layer top-side down on plate.

Spread 1/2 to 3/4 cup (125 to 175 mL) frosting on cake. Place second cake layer, top-side up over frosting. You now have the two flat surfaces together in the center so the cakes will sit evenly.

Spread a very thin layer of frosting on top and sides of cake. This seals in crumbs. Then cover with a second, thicker layer of frosting. You can smooth the surface with a long spatula or make swirls with a small spatula or the back of a spoon.

Chill cake if necessary to firm up frosting. Carefully remove waxed paper strips.

Cakes baked in 13- by 9-inch (3.5 L) pans are usually glazed or frosted and served right from the pan.

For cakes, that are brushed with a syrup while warm (usually tube and Bundt cakes), put cake on rack over waxed paper to catch the drips.

Dusting with confectioner's sugar is a simple yet attractive finish to plain cakes. Do this just before serving since as the moisture from the cake will absorb the dusting quickly. For an elegant or festive look, place a doily over cake, sprinkle generously with confectioner's sugar and remove doily.

Quick glaze. Microwave a ready-to-serve frosting for about 40 seconds, or just to warm slightly, stirring until a shiny, thick, pourable consistency is reached. Pour over cake and leave to harden.

STORING CAKES

Properly wrapped, cake keeps very well. You can refrigerate most cakes up to a week or freeze them 4 to 6 months.

Cool unfrosted cakes completely before freezing. Having a few plain cake layers in the freezer is a bonus. You can thaw, fill and frost in no time when necessary.

Chill or freeze frosted cake for about 30 minutes to harden frosting so it doesn't stick to the wrapping.

THAWING CAKES

Thaw frosted cakes overnight in the refrigerator if the frosting contains eggs or cream. Thaw other cakes the same way, or at room temperature, for about 3 hours.

For unfrosted cakes that are going to be frosted, leave covered about three-quarters of thawing time then uncover for the remaining time so they dry out slightly for easy frosting.

HIGH-ALTITUDE BAKING

At high altitudes, over 3500 feet (1000 m), there is less air pressure and humidity. Both these factors can drastically affect cake baking. Lower air pressure can cause cakes to overflow or collapse. Don't fill the pans more than half full with batter. It also helps to use eggs that are cold rather than at the usual room temperature. You should add 2 tbsp (25 mL) flour to toughen the cakes a little. Increase the oven temperature by 25° F (10° C) to set the batter before it over-rises. If given a choice, use the larger pan size suggested. Cakes also tend to stick to the pans more. Be sure to grease the pans generously before dusting with flour.

SINGLE-LAYER CAKES

Chocolate Peanut Butter and Banana Cake

Preheat oven to 350° F (180° C)

13- by 9-inch (3.5 L) cake pan, greased and floured

Serves 12 to 16

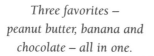

*Three favorites –
peanut butter, banana and
chocolate – all in one.*

Use creamy peanut butter,
not crunchy, for a smooth,
satiny glaze.

Keep this glaze in mind for other
cakes and squares as well.

VARIATION

Omit glaze and frost with
BANANA BUTTER FROSTING (see
recipe, page 163).

Cake

1	pkg (18.25 oz [515 g]) devil's food cake mix	1
3	eggs	3
1 1/2 cups	mashed ripe bananas (3 or 4 large bananas)	375 mL
1/2 cup	vegetable oil	125 mL

Chocolate Peanut Butter Glaze

4	squares (each 1 oz [28 g]) semi-sweet chocolate	4
2/3 cup	creamy peanut butter	150 mL
1/3 cup	chopped peanuts (optional)	75 mL

1. *Cake:* In a large mixer bowl, combine cake mix, eggs, mashed bananas and oil. Beat on medium speed for 2 minutes, or until smooth. Spread batter evenly in prepared pan. Bake 35 to 40 minutes or until a toothpick inserted in center comes out clean. Cool completely in pan on a wire rack.

2. *Glaze:* In a small saucepan over low heat, melt chocolate and peanut butter, stirring constantly until smooth. Spread evenly over cooled cake. Sprinkle nuts on top, if desired.

Fruit Cocktail Cake

Preheat oven to 350° F (180° C)
13- by 9-inch (3.5 L) cake pan, greased

Serves 12 to 16

*The taste will vary
with different brands of
fruit cocktail.*

TIP

Put coconut topping on in blobs.
Don't try to spread it over the
nuts. The blobs give the cake a
unique look when cooled.

VARIATION

If maraschino cherries aren't a
favorite, you can leave them out.

Use vanilla pudding mix in
place of lemon.

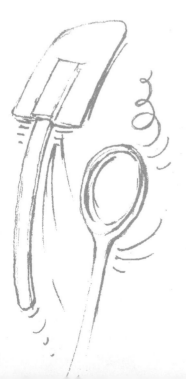

Cake

1	pkg (18.25 oz [515 g]) white cake mix	1
1	pkg (4-serving size) lemon instant pudding mix	1
3/4 cup	flaked coconut	175 mL
4	eggs	4
1/3 cup	vegetable oil	75 mL
1	can (14 oz [398 mL]) fruit cocktail, with juice	1
1/4 cup	chopped maraschino cherries	50 mL

Nut Topping

2/3 cup	chopped pecans	150 mL
1/2 cup	packed brown sugar	125 mL

Coconut Topping

1/2 cup	granulated sugar	125 mL
1/2 cup	butter	125 mL
1/2 cup	light (10%) cream	125 mL
1 cup	flaked coconut	250 mL

1. *Cake:* In a large mixer bowl, combine cake mix, pudding mix, coconut, eggs, oil and fruit cocktail with juice. Beat on medium speed for 2 minutes. Stir in cherries. Spread batter evenly in prepared pan.

2. *Nut Topping:* Combine nuts and brown sugar. Sprinkle evenly over batter. Bake 45 to 50 minutes or until a toothpick inserted in center comes out clean.

3. *Coconut Topping:* (Prepare at the end of cake baking time.) In a small saucepan, combine sugar, butter and cream. Bring to a boil over medium heat, then boil for 2 minutes. Stir in coconut. Spoon blobs of topping randomly over hot cake. Cool completely in pan on a wire rack before cutting.

Take-Along Cake

Preheat oven to 350° F (180° C)
13- by 9-inch (3.5 L) cake pan, greased

Serves 12 to 16

Ideal for family picnics. A one-step cake with a frosting that bakes along with the cake.

TIP

Store chocolate in a cool dry place. If storage area is warm, chocolate develops a gray coating called "bloom." Bloom has no effect on the flavor or quality of the chocolate and will disappear during baking.

VARIATION

Use your favorite chocolate-flavored cake mix.

1	pkg (18.25 oz [515 g]) milk or Swiss chocolate cake mix	1
1 cup	miniature semi-sweet chocolate chips	250 mL
1 cup	miniature marshmallows	250 mL
1/4 cup	butter, melted	50 mL
1/2 cup	packed brown sugar	125 mL
1/2 cup	chopped pecans or walnuts	125 mL

1. Prepare cake mix according to package directions. Stir in chocolate chips and marshmallows. Spread batter evenly in prepared pan. Drizzle melted butter evenly over batter. Sprinkle brown sugar and nuts on top. Bake 40 to 50 minutes or until a toothpick inserted in center comes out clean. Cool at least 30 minutes in pan on a wire rack before cutting.

Chocolate Mayonnaise Cake

Preheat oven to 350° F (180° C)
13- by 9-inch (3.5 L) cake pan, greased

Serves 12 to 16

*Mayonnaise adds richness
to an already moist cake.*

1	pkg (18.25 oz [515 g]) devil's food cake mix	1
3	eggs	3
1 1/3 cups	milk	325 mL
1 cup	mayonnaise	250 mL
1/2 tsp	ground cinnamon (optional)	2 mL

1. In a large mixer bowl, combine cake mix, eggs, milk, mayonnaise and cinnamon. Beat on medium speed for 2 minutes or until smooth. Spread batter evenly in prepared pan. Bake 35 to 40 minutes or until a toothpick inserted in center comes out clean. Cool completely in pan on a wire rack. Frost as desired.

TIP

You can replace water with milk in cake mixes for added nutrition. Keep in mind that it lightens the color of darker cakes.

VARIATION

The hint of cinnamon is a personal preference. Omit it if it's not to your liking. You can also replace the milk with coffee or water.

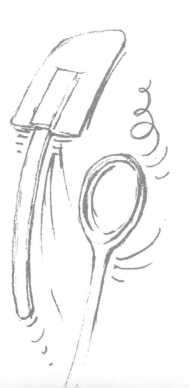

Chocolate Praline Cake

Preheat oven to 350° F (180° C)
13- by 9-inch (3.5 L) cake pan, greased

Serves 12 to 16

*The broiled topping here –
or on almost any cake –
makes it a guaranteed
success.*

1	pkg (18.25 oz [515 g]) devil's food cake mix	1
2	eggs	2
1 1/4 cups	water	300 mL
1/3 cup	vegetable oil	75 mL
	CRUNCHY BROILED TOPPING (see recipe, page 173)	

1. In a large mixer bowl, combine cake mix, eggs, water and oil. Beat on medium speed for 2 minutes. Spread batter evenly in prepared pan. Bake 35 to 40 minutes or until a toothpick inserted in center comes out clean. Cool 5 to 10 minutes, then complete with broiled topping. Cool completely in pan on a wire rack before cutting.

TIP

Broiled toppings burn quickly
so watch constantly
while broiling.

VARIATION

The topping also works well on
white, yellow and spice
cakes.

Triple Lemon Cake

Preheat oven to 350° F (180° C)
13- by 9-inch (3.5 L) cake pan, greased

Serves 12 to 16

This may not be the most attractive cake but it definitely is the most lemony. Being a lemon fanatic, it's one of my favorites.

TIP

If you leave this cake 20 minutes before glazing, the glaze will harden to look like a white icing, with a bit of a crunch. Reduce the cooling time to only 10 minutes and the glaze sinks in, leaving a softer, shiny top. I'm not sure which I prefer. I love them both.

VARIATION

For a more mellow lemon flavor, try a lemon instant pudding or use the lemon gelatin with a white cake mix.

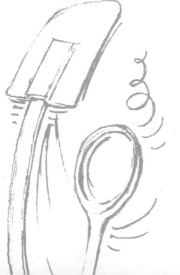

Cake

1	pkg (18.25 oz [515 g]) lemon cake mix	1
1	pkg (3 oz [85 g]) lemon-flavored gelatin dessert mix	1
4	eggs	4
3/4 cup	vegetable oil	175 mL
3/4 cup	water	175 mL

Glaze

2 cups	confectioner's (icing) sugar, sifted	500 mL
1/3 cup	lemon juice	75 mL

1. *Cake:* In a large mixer bowl, combine cake mix, gelatin mix, eggs, oil and water. Beat on medium speed for 4 minutes. Spread batter evenly in prepared pan. Bake 35 to 40 minutes or until a toothpick inserted in center comes out clean. Cool for about 20 minutes (see Tip, at left).

2. *Glaze:* Poke holes with tines of fork about 1-inch (2.5 cm) apart on top of warm cake. Whisk confectioner's sugar and lemon juice together until sugar dissolves. Pour evenly over warm cake. Cool completely in pan on a wire rack before cutting.

Mississippi Mud Cake

Preheat oven to 350° F (180° C)
13- by 9-inch (3.5 L) cake pan, greased

Serves 12 to 16

Marshmallows are always a hit with kids, young and old.

Cake

1	pkg (18.25 oz [515 g]) devil's food cake mix	1
4	eggs	4
1 cup	sour cream	250 mL
1/2 cup	cold strong black coffee	125 mL
1/2 cup	vegetable oil	125 mL

Topping

3 cups	miniature marshmallows	750 mL
1 cup	chopped pecans	250 mL

Chocolate Drizzle

3	squares (each 1 oz [28 g]) semi-sweet chocolate	3
3 tbsp	butter	45 mL

1. *Cake:* In a large mixer bowl, combine cake mix, eggs, sour cream, coffee and oil. Beat on medium speed for 2 minutes or until smooth. Spread batter evenly in prepared pan. Bake 35 to 40 minutes or until a toothpick inserted in center comes out clean.

2. *Topping:* Sprinkle marshmallows and nuts over cake as soon as it comes out of oven. Bake 5 minutes longer or until marshmallows puff. Remove from oven. Cool 30 minutes in pan on a wire rack.

3. *Drizzle:* In a small saucepan over low heat, melt chocolate and butter or microwave on Medium for 2 minutes. Stir until smooth. Drizzle over marshmallow-nut layer. Serve warm or cool to room temperature before cutting.

Peach of a Peach Cake

Preheat oven to 350° F (180° C)
13- by 9-inch (3.5 L) cake pan, greased

Serves 12 to 16

A great cake to take to your next pot-luck party.

Use pie filling directly from can. If necessary, chop any large peach pieces.

Omit lemon extract in cake if desired.

Cake

1	pkg (18.25 oz [515 g]) white cake mix	1
1/4 cup	all-purpose flour	50 mL
1 tsp	baking powder	5 mL
3	eggs	3
1	can (19 oz [540 mL]) peach or peach-and-passion-fruit pie filling	1
1/2 tsp	lemon extract	2 mL
1/2 cup	chopped walnuts	125 mL

Topping

1/2 cup	granulated sugar	125 mL
1/2 cup	all-purpose flour	125 mL
3/4 tsp	ground cinnamon	3 mL
1/4 cup	butter, softened	50 mL

1. *Cake:* In a large mixer bowl, combine cake mix, flour, baking powder, eggs, pie filling, lemon extract and nuts. Beat on medium speed for 2 minutes or until well blended. Spread batter evenly in prepared pan.

2. *Topping:* In a small bowl, combine sugar, flour and cinnamon. With a pastry blender or a fork, cut in butter until crumbly. Sprinkle evenly over batter. Bake 40 to 45 minutes or until a toothpick inserted in center comes out clean. Cool at least 30 minutes in pan on wire rack before cutting.

Carrot Cake with Raisins

Preheat oven to 350° F (180° C)
13- by 9-inch (3.5 L) cake pan, greased

Serves 12 to 16

This is the choice of carrot cakes for those who like raisins and don't have a can of crushed pineapple on hand. The pudding mix gives it a different taste to PINEAPPLE CARROT CAKE *(see recipe, page 35). Try them both and choose a favorite. We couldn't decide.*

1	pkg (18.25 oz [515 g]) white cake mix	1
1	pkg (4-serving size) vanilla instant pudding mix	1
4	eggs	4
2 cups	grated peeled carrots	500 mL
1/3 cup	vegetable oil	75 mL
1/4 cup	water	50 mL
3/4 cup	raisins	175 mL
2 tsp	ground cinnamon	10 mL
1/2 tsp	ground nutmeg	2 mL

1. In a large mixer bowl, combine cake mix, pudding mix, eggs, carrots, oil, water, raisins, cinnamon and nutmeg. Beat on low speed for 1 minute to blend, then on medium speed for 2 minutes. Spread batter in prepared pan. Bake 40 to 45 minutes or until a toothpick inserted in center comes out clean. Cool completely in pan on a wire rack.

TIP

If raisins have dried in storage, plump them in boiling water about 5 minutes then drain well and pat dry.

Top with your favorite cream cheese frosting.

VARIATION

Try dried cranberries in place of raisins.

French Apple Upside-Down Cake

Preheat oven to 350° F (180° C)
13- by 9-inch (3.5 L) cake pan, greased

Serves 12 to 16

Enjoy upside-down cakes with fresh fruit while it's in season; try the canned fruit versions later on.

TIP

If peeling apples ahead, toss with a little lemon juice to prevent browning.

Whipped cream or ice cream is a delicious addition to this dessert.

VARIATION

Try a spice or yellow cake mix another time.

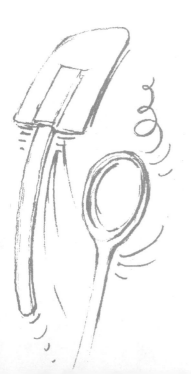

Topping

4 cups	peeled, cored and sliced apples (4 or 5 large apples)	1 L
2/3 cup	granulated sugar	175 mL
1 tbsp	all-purpose flour	15 mL
1 tsp	ground cinnamon	5 mL
2 tbsp	butter, melted	25 mL
2 tbsp	lemon juice	25 mL

Cake

1	pkg (18.25 oz [515 g]) white cake mix	1
3	eggs	3
1 1/4 cups	water	300 mL
1/3 cup	vegetable oil	75 mL

1. *Topping:* Arrange apple slices in prepared pan. Combine sugar, flour and cinnamon. Sprinkle over apples. Combine melted butter and lemon juice. Drizzle over apples.

2. *Cake:* In a large mixer bowl, combine cake mix, eggs, water and oil. Beat on medium speed for 2 minutes. Pour batter evenly over fruit mixture. Bake 40 to 50 minutes or until a toothpick inserted in center comes out clean. Let stand 5 minutes, then turn upside down onto a large platter or a cookie sheet. Serve warm.

Pineapple Upside-Down Cake

Preheat oven to 350° F (180° C)
13- by 9-inch (3.5 L) cake pan

Serves 12 to 16

It's always amazing when something so simple can look so beautiful. This cake certainly has passed the test of time and will always be a favorite.

TIP

Although I prefer the flavor of butter in baking, you can also use hard margarine – but not the soft or diet type spreads.

Tilt pan to distribute melted butter evenly over the bottom.

VARIATION

Canned peach slices or apricot halves also look attractive on this cake.

1/3 cup	butter	75 mL
1 cup	packed brown sugar	250 mL
1	can (19 oz [540 mL]) pineapple rings (about 12 rings) drained, juice reserved	1
12	maraschino cherries (optional)	12
1	pkg (18.25 oz [515 g]) white cake mix	1
3	eggs	3
2/3 cup	reserved pineapple juice	150 mL
2/3 cup	water	150 mL
1/3 cup	vegetable oil	75 mL
	Whipped cream (optional)	

1. Melt butter in cake pan. Sprinkle brown sugar evenly over top. Arrange drained pineapple slices over sugar. Place a cherry in center of each ring, if desired.

2. In a large mixer bowl, combine cake mix, eggs, pineapple juice, water and oil. Beat on medium speed for 2 minutes. Pour batter evenly over fruit. Bake 45 to 50 minutes or until a toothpick inserted in center comes out clean. Let stand 5 minutes, then turn upside down onto a large platter or a cookie sheet. Serve warm with a generous dollop of whipped cream, if desired.

Banana Pudding Cake

Preheat oven to 350° F (180° C)
13- by 9-inch (3.5 L) cake pan, greased

Serves 12 to 16

*Very simple and very good.
Add a broiled topping,
as we've done here, a
banana butter icing or
just leave plain.*

1	pkg (18.25 oz [515 g]) white cake mix	1
1	pkg (4-serving size) vanilla instant pudding mix	1
4	eggs	4
1 1/2 cups	mashed ripe bananas (3 or 4 large bananas)	375 mL
1/3 cup	vegetable oil	75 mL
	CRUNCHY BROILED TOPPING (see recipe, page 173)	

1. In a large mixer bowl, combine cake mix, pudding mix, eggs, mashed bananas and oil. Beat on medium speed for 2 minutes or until smooth. Spread batter evenly in prepared pan. Bake 35 to 40 minutes or until a toothpick inserted in center comes out clean. Top with broiled topping. Cool at least 30 minutes in pan on a wire rack before cutting.

TIP

Cakes baked in this size pan are usually frosted and served from the pan. It's a wise choice if you have to transport the cake somewhere. If you want to remove the entire cake, line pan with foil, leaving side overhangs. You can lift the cooled cake out of pan easily with the foil.

VARIATION

A butterscotch or chocolate pudding makes an interesting combination with banana.

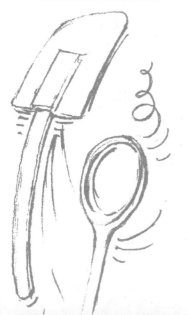

Rainbow Dessert Cake

Preheat oven to 350° F (180° C)
13- by 9-inch (3.5 L) cake pan, greased

Serves 12 to 16

A colorful cake that's always popular at children's birthdays.

TIP

After removing from the oven be sure to let cake stand no more than 20 minutes before topping.

Start preparing gelatin mixture as soon as you put cake in the oven.

The topping is a personal taste. You can use real whipped cream, lightly sweetened, if you prefer.

VARIATION

Your choice of gelatin will dictate the color. We found red, green and purple to be favorites with kids.

Cake

1	pkg (18.25 oz [515 g]) white cake mix	1

Topping

1	pkg (3 oz [85 g]) gelatin dessert mix, any flavor	1
3/4 cup	boiling water	175 mL
1/2 cup	cold water	125 mL
2 cups	prepared dessert topping or sweetened whipped cream	500 mL
	Rainbow-colored cake sprinkles (optional)	

1. *Cake:* Prepare and bake cake according to package directions for 13- by 9-inch (3.5 L) pan. Cool cake 20 minutes in pan on a wire rack.

2. *Topping:* Prepare topping as soon as you put cake into the oven. In a small bowl, add boiling water to gelatin. Stir well until gelatin crystals are completely dissolved. Stir in cold water. Set aside at room temperature. Poke deep holes about 1-inch (2.5 cm) apart through the top of cake with a fork. Slowly pour gelatin mixture evenly over surface of cake. Chill thoroughly, about 1 hour. Cover cake with whipped topping. Scatter sprinkles on top, if desired. Chill until serving. Store leftover cake in refrigerator.

Mix-in-the-Pan Cherry Cake

Serves 12 to 16

The fascinating appearance comes from swirling a pie filling through the cake batter just before baking.

Preheat oven to 350° F (180° C)
13- by 9-inch (3.5 L) cake pan

1/4 cup	vegetable oil	50 mL
1	pkg (18.25 oz [515 g]) white cake mix	1
2	eggs	2
1/2 cup	water	125 mL
1	can (19 oz [540 mL]) cherry pie filling	1

1. Pour oil into pan. Tilt pan to coat bottom with oil. Sprinkle dry cake mix evenly on top. Add eggs and water. Stir all together with a fork or spoon until thoroughly blended, about 2 minutes. Scrape sides and spread batter evenly in pan. Drop spoonfuls of pie filling randomly on top. With a fork or knife, fold pie filling into batter just enough to create a marble effect. Bake 35 to 40 minutes or until a toothpick inserted in center comes out clean. Cool cake at least 30 minutes in pan on a wire rack before cutting.

TIP

Swirl the pie filling gently. Overmixing will result in a red cherry cake with no marbling.

Sprinkle cooled cake with confectioner's (icing) sugar or serve warm with ice cream, custard or vanilla sauce.

Soften a good quality French vanilla ice cream to a pouring consistency for an extremely easy and wonderful tasting sauce.

VARIATION

Color and flavor will depend on the pie filling. Try your favorite.

Lemon Pop Cake with Pineapple Coconut Topping

Preheat oven to 350° F (180° C)
13- by 9-inch (3.5 L) cake pan, greased and floured

Serves 12 to 16

The pop is in the cake; it's not the cake that "pops."

TIP

Have the soda pop at room temperature when preparing the cake.

VARIATION

You can prepare the cake and freeze it. When you want a quick dessert, thaw the cake and add the topping.

Cake

1	pkg (18.25 oz [515 g]) lemon cake mix	1
1	pkg (4-serving size) lemon instant pudding mix	1
4	eggs	4
2/3 cup	vegetable oil	150 mL
1 cup	lemon-lime soda	250 mL

Pineapple Coconut Topping

2 cups	frozen whipped topping, thawed	500 mL
1/2 cup	well-drained crushed pineapple	125 mL
1/2 cup	toasted coconut	125 mL

1. *Cake:* In a large mixer bowl, combine cake mix, pudding mix, eggs and oil. Beat on medium speed for 3 minutes. Gradually add soda, beating on low speed until smooth, then beat on medium speed for 1 minute longer. Spread batter evenly in prepared pan. Bake 30 to 40 minutes or until a toothpick inserted in center comes out clean. Cool completely in pan on a wire rack.

2. *Topping:* Gently fold pineapple and coconut into whipped topping. Spread over cooled cake. Chill until serving. Store leftover cake in refrigerator.

Lemon Cream Dessert Cake

Preheat oven to 350° F (180° C)
13- by 9-inch (3.5 L) cake pan, greased

Serves 12 to 16

A refreshing light dessert to enjoy all summer long.

TIP

Prepare gelatin mixture as soon as you put cake in the oven. Leave gelatin mixture at room temperature while cake bakes. Chilling will make it set too quickly.

Be sure to let cake stand just 20 minutes after baking before pouring gelatin mixture over.

VARIATION

If you love lemon, use lemon cake mix.

Cake

1	pkg (18.25 oz [515 g]) yellow or white cake mix	1

Topping

1	pkg (3 oz [85 g]) lemon flavored gelatin dessert mix	1
3/4 cup	boiling water	175 mL
1/2 cup	cold water	125 mL
1	envelope (1.3 oz [42.5 g]) whipped topping mix	1
1	pkg (4-serving size) lemon instant pudding mix	1
1 1/2 cups	cold milk	375 mL

1. *Cake:* Prepare and bake cake according to package directions for 13- by 9-inch (3.5 L) pan. Cool cake in pan on a wire rack 20 minutes.

2. *Topping:* Prepare topping as soon as you put cake into the oven. In a small bowl, add boiling water to gelatin. Stir well until gelatin crystals are completely dissolved. Stir in cold water. Set aside at room temperature. Poke deep holes about 1-inch (2.5 cm) apart through top of cake with fork. Slowly pour gelatin mixture evenly over surface of cake. Chill thoroughly, about 1 hour. In a small bowl, blend topping mix, pudding mix and milk then beat on high speed for about 5 minutes or until stiff peaks form. Spread evenly over cake. Chill until serving. Store leftover cake in refrigerator.

Candy Bar Cake

Preheat oven to 350° F (180° C)
13- by 9-inch (3.5 L) cake pan, greased

Serves 12 to 16

A cake version of an all-time favorite, chocolate caramel pecan candy.

Filling

1 lb	caramels (about 65 caramels)	500 g
1/2 cup	evaporated milk	125 mL

Cake

1	pkg (18.25 oz [515 g]) devil's food cake mix	1
1	pkg (4-serving size) chocolate instant pudding mix	1
4	eggs	4
1 cup	sour cream	250 mL
1/2 cup	vegetable oil	125 mL
1/4 cup	water	50 mL

Topping

2 cups	semi-sweet chocolate chips	500 mL
1 3/4 cups	chopped pecans	425 mL
2 tbsp	butter	25 mL

1. *Filling:* In a saucepan over low heat, heat caramels and evaporated milk, stirring often until smoothly melted. Keep warm while preparing cake.

2. *Cake:* In a large mixer bowl, combine cake mix, pudding mix, eggs, sour cream, oil and water. Beat on medium speed for 2 minutes. Spread half of batter evenly in prepared pan. Bake 15 minutes or just until set. Pour caramel mixture evenly over top.

3. *Topping:* Sprinkle 1 cup (250 mL) chocolate chips and 1 cup (250 mL) pecans over caramel layer. Carefully spread remaining cake batter over filling. Bake 35 to 40 minutes longer. Cool 30 minutes in pan on a wire rack before glazing. In a small saucepan over low heat, melt remaining 1 cup (250 mL) chocolate chips and butter or microwave on medium for 2 minutes, stirring until smooth. Spread over cake. Sprinkle with remaining 3/4 cup (175 mL) pecans. Cool completely before cutting.

PINEAPPLE CARROT CAKE (PAGE 35) ➤

Chocolate Cherry Cake

Preheat oven to 350° F (180° C)
13- by 9-inch (3.5 L) cake pan, greased

Serves 12 to 16

It's hard to believe the pie filling replaces the usual fat and liquid ingredients in a cake mix. But it works — very well too! With the mix and pie filling on hand it's an easy last-minute cake to prepare.

Cake

1	pkg (18.25 oz [515 g]) devil's food cake mix	1
1	can (19 oz/ [540 mL]) cherry pie filling	1
2	eggs	2

Chocolate Glaze

3/4 cup	granulated sugar	175 mL
1/4 cup	butter	50 mL
1/4 cup	light (10%) cream	50 mL
3/4 cup	semi-sweet chocolate chips	175 mL
1/4 tsp	almond extract	1 mL
	Sliced almonds, toasted (optional)	

1. *Cake:* In a large mixer bowl, combine cake mix, pie filling and eggs. Beat on medium speed for 2 minutes. Spread batter evenly in prepared pan. Bake 30 to 40 minutes or until a toothpick inserted in center comes out clean. Cool 30 minutes in pan on a wire rack before glazing.

2. *Glaze:* In a small saucepan, combine sugar, butter and cream. Cook, stirring constantly over medium heat until mixture comes to a boil, then boil for 1 minute. Remove from heat. Add chocolate chips and extract, stirring until smoothly melted. Spread over warm cake. Cool completely before cutting.

◄ BUMBLEBERRY LEMON UPSIDE-DOWN CAKE (PAGE 36)

Chocolate Cola Cake

Preheat oven to 350° F (180° C)
13- by 9-inch (3.5 L) cake pan, greased

Serves 12 to 16

Some like cola with chocolate cake. Now you can enjoy it in the cake with a glass of cold milk.

TIP

Use cola at room temperature – not cold, as you would for drinking.

The addition of cocoa to a white cake gives it the flavor of a chocolate cake mix. Be sure to sift the cocoa before using, since it tends to clump in storage.

VARIATION

The frosting is delicious with or without nuts.

Cake

1	pkg (18.25 oz [515 g]) white cake mix	1
1/3 cup	cocoa, sifted	75 mL
2	eggs	2
1 cup	cola	250 mL
1/2 cup	milk	125 mL
1/2 cup	vegetable oil	125 mL
1 1/3 cups	miniature marshmallows	325 mL

Chocolate Cola Frosting

1/2 cup	butter	125 mL
1/3 cup	cocoa, sifted	75 mL
1/3 cup	cola	75 mL
2 3/4 cups to 3 cups	confectioners (icing) sugar, sifted	675 mL to 750 mL
3/4 cup	chopped peanuts (optional)	175 mL

1. *Cake:* In a large mixer bowl, combine cake mix, cocoa, eggs, cola, milk and oil. Beat on medium speed for 2 minutes. Fold in marshmallows. Spread batter evenly in prepared pan. Bake 40 to 45 minutes or until top springs back when lightly touched. (The toothpick test may not work if it touches the marshmallows.) Cool 1 hour in pan on a wire rack before frosting.

2. *Frosting:* In a medium saucepan, melt butter. Add cocoa and cola, stirring until smooth. Bring to a boil, stirring constantly. Remove from heat. Gradually add enough confectioners sugar, stirring, to make a smooth spreading consistency. Stir in nuts, if desired. Spread evenly over cake. Cool completely before cutting.

Pineapple Carrot Cake

Preheat oven to 350° F (180° C)
13- by 9-inch (3.5 L) cake pan, greased

Serves 12 to 16

*Taste testers couldn't decide
between this carrot cake
with pineapple and CARROT
CAKE WITH RAISINS (see
recipe, page 24) so I've
included them both. Top
with traditional CREAM
CHEESE FROSTING (see
recipe, page 170) or another
family favorite.*

1	pkg (18.25 oz [515 g]) white cake mix	1
4	eggs	4
2 cups	peeled, grated carrots	500 mL
1 cup	undrained crushed pineapple	250 mL
1/2 cup	vegetable oil	125 mL
1/4 cup	water	50 mL
2 tsp	ground cinnamon	10 mL
1/4 tsp	ground nutmeg	1 mL

1. In a large mixer bowl, combine cake mix, eggs, carrots, pineapple with juice, oil, water, cinnamon and nutmeg. Beat on low speed for 1 minute to blend, then on medium speed for 2 minutes or until well blended. Spread batter evenly in prepared pan. Bake 35 to 40 minutes or until a toothpick inserted in center comes out clean. Cool completely in pan on a wire rack. Frost as desired.

TIP

Look for crisp large carrots.
They're easier to peel and grate.

VARIATION

A yellow cake mix gives the
cake a golden color and a
different flavor from white.

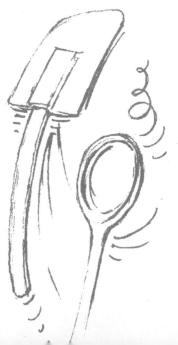

Bumbleberry Lemon Upside-Down Cake

Preheat oven to 350° F (180° C)
13- by 9-inch (3.5 L) cake pan

Serves 12 to 16

Bumbleberry is a mixture of fruits. Use your favorites, or what is in season.

1/3 cup	butter	75 mL
1 cup	packed brown sugar	250 mL
1 1/2 cups	fresh raspberries	375 mL
1 1/2 cups	fresh blueberries	375 mL
1 cup	fresh strawberries	250 mL
1	pkg (18.25 oz [515 g]) lemon cake mix	1
	Whipped cream (optional)	

1. In cake pan, melt butter. Sprinkle brown sugar evenly on top. Scatter fruit over sugar.

2. Prepare cake mix according to package directions. Pour batter evenly over fruit. Bake 45 to 50 minutes or until a toothpick inserted in center of cake comes out clean. Let stand 5 minutes, then turn upside down onto a large platter or a cookie sheet. Serve warm with a generous dollop of whipped cream, if desired.

MULTI-LAYER CAKES

Pineapple Mandarin Cake

Preheat oven to 350° F (180° C)
Two 9-inch (1.5 L) round cake pans, greased and floured

Serves 12 to 16

Sometimes the simple cakes are the best. Although easy to prepare with just a few ingredients, the flavor and appearance of this cake is wonderful.

1	pkg (18.25 oz [515 g]) white cake mix	1
3	eggs	3
1	can (10 oz [284 mL]) mandarin oranges, drained, liquid reserved	1
1	can (10 oz [284 mL]) crushed pineapple, drained, liquid reserved	1
1 1/3 cups	reserved fruit juice (from above), plus water as necessary	325 mL
1/3 cup	vegetable oil	75 mL
	Lemon BUTTER FROSTING (see recipe, page 161)	

1. *Cake:* In a large mixer bowl, combine cake mix, eggs, juice mixture and oil. Beat on medium speed for 2 minutes. Spread batter in prepared pans, dividing evenly. Bake 30 to 35 minutes or until a toothpick inserted in center comes out clean. Cool cakes 10 minutes in pans, then remove to a wire rack and cool completely.

2. *Assembly:* Prepare BASIC LEMON BUTTER FROSTING. Place 1 cake layer top-side down on a serving plate. Spread with a generous amount of frosting. Put remaining cake layer top-side up over frosting. Cover top and sides of cake completely with remaining frosting. Decorate top of cake with a ring of drained mandarin segments around outside. Fill center with well-drained pineapple. Decorate center with a few mandarins. Chill until serving. Store leftover cake in refrigerator.

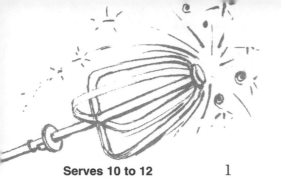

Crunch 'n' Cream Chocolate Torte

Preheat oven to 350° F (180° C)
Two 9-inch (1.5 L) round cake pans, greased and floured

Serves 10 to 12

I like to use Skor chocolate bars for this cake, but you may have another favorite.

1	pkg (18.25 oz [515 g]) devil's food cake mix	1
	CHOCOLATE WHIPPED CREAM FILLING (see recipe, page 176)	
4	toffee-crunch chocolate bars (each 1.4 oz [39 g]), crushed	4

1. *Cake:* Prepare and bake cake according to package directions to make two 9-inch (23 cm) round cake layers. Cool in pans on a wire rack 10 minutes, then remove layers and cool completely. With a long, sharp knife, cut each layer horizontally in half to make 4 layers.

2. *Filling:* Prepare Chocolate Whipped Cream Filling. Fold in three-quarters of the crushed chocolate bars.

3. *Assembly:* Place 1 halved cake layer on a serving plate. Spread with one-quarter of the filling. Repeat layering with remaining cake layers and filling. Sprinkle remaining crushed chocolate bar on top. Chill until serving. Store leftover cake in refrigerator.

Chocolate Orange Jubilee Cake

Preheat oven to 350° F (180° C)

Three 8-inch (1.2 L) or 9-inch (1.5 L) round cake pans

Serves about 12

A creamy orange frosting nestled between six layers of feathery light chocolate cake.

TIP

If your oven won't hold 3 pans on one shelf, put 2 on the upper middle rack and one on a lower rack. Change positions halfway through baking.

Cake

1	pkg (18.25 oz [515 g]) devil's food cake mix	1
3	eggs	3
2/3 cup	orange juice	150 mL
2/3 cup	water	150 mL
1/3 cup	vegetable oil	75 mL
1 tbsp	grated orange zest	15 mL

Orange Buttercream Filling & Frosting

1 1/2 cups	butter, softened	375 mL
2 tbsp	orange juice	25 mL
1 tbsp	grated orange zest	15 mL
4 cups	confectioner's (icing) sugar, sifted	1 L
2	egg yolks	2
	Chocolate curls or shaved chocolate	
	Orange slices, candied or fresh	

1. *Cake:* In a large mixer bowl, combine cake mix, eggs, orange juice, water, oil and zest. Beat on medium speed for 2 minutes. Spread batter in prepared pans, dividing evenly. Bake 20 to 30 minutes or until a toothpick inserted in center comes out clean. Cool 10 minutes in pans on a wire rack then remove layers and cool completely. With a long, sharp knife, cut each layer horizontally in half to make 6 layers.

2. *Filling & Frosting:* In a large mixer bowl, beat butter, orange juice and zest on medium speed until creamy. Gradually add confectioner's sugar and egg yolks, beating until smooth and fluffy.

3. *Assembly:* Spread buttercream between each layer, placing one on top of the other on a serving plate. Frost sides and top of cake, reserving some for decoration. Decorate top of cake with rosettes of buttercream, chocolate curls and orange slices. Chill until serving. If using fresh orange slices, place on cake just before serving.

Triple Chocolate Fudge Cake

Preheat oven to 350° F (180° C)
Two 9-inch (1.5 L) round cake pans, greased and floured

Serves about 10 to 12

The chocolate lover's dream.

Cake

1	pkg (18.25 oz [515 g]) devil's food cake mix	1
1 tbsp	instant coffee powder	15 mL
3	eggs	3
1 cup	water	250 mL
1/2 cup	sour cream	125 mL
1/3 cup	vegetable oil	75 mL

Filling

1/2 cup	butter, softened	125 mL
3 1/2 cups	confectioner's (icing) sugar, sifted	825 mL
1/2 cup	light (10%) cream	125 mL
2	squares (each 1 oz [28 g]) unsweetened chocolate, melted and cooled	2

Glaze

4	squares (each 1 oz [28 g]) semi-sweet chocolate	4
2 tbsp	strong coffee	25 mL
3 tbsp	butter, softened	45 mL

1. *Cake:* In a large mixer bowl, combine cake mix, coffee powder, eggs, water, sour cream and oil. Beat on medium speed for 2 minutes. Spread in prepared pans, dividing evenly. Bake 30 to 35 minutes or until a toothpick inserted in center comes out clean. Cool 10 minutes in pans on a wire rack, then remove layers and cool completely.

2. *Filling:* Beat all ingredients together on medium speed until light and fluffy. Add more confectioner's sugar or cream to make a soft, creamy spreading consistency.

3. *Assembly:* Place 1 cake layer top-side down on a serving plate. Spread with a generous amount of filling. Place second cake layer on top. Spread remaining filling on sides of cake, leaving top unfrosted. Chill 30 minutes.

4. *Glaze:* In a small saucepan over low heat, melt chocolate and coffee, stirring until smooth. Remove from heat. Gradually add butter, stirring until smooth. Spread over top of cake, letting it drip down sides. Chill to set chocolate glaze.

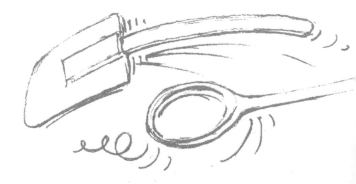

Strawberry Meringue Shortcake

Preheat oven to 350° F (180° C)
Two 9-inch (1.5 L) round cake pans and one 8-inch (20 cm) or 9-inch (23 cm) round
or square pan, greased and lined with waxed paper or parchment in bottom

Serves 10 to 12

A real showpiece. The almond meringue topping and cake bake together, leaving only the filling to add.

TIP

You'll need 3 pans for this recipe. Two rounds for the shortcake and another for leftover batter which the family can enjoy.

Buy extra fruit to scatter on the plate around the cake for a stunning presentation.

For neat, easy removal of cakes from pans, loosen edge with a knife then turn over on a tea-towel-covered board. Remove paper and turn over right-side up on rack.

VARIATION

Other fruits work well. Try raspberries, blueberries and peach slices – or any other colorful combination of fruits.

Cake		
1	pkg (18.25 oz [515 g]) princess white cake mix	1
4	egg yolks	4
1 1/8 cups	water	275 mL
2 tbsp	vegetable oil	25 mL

Meringue Topping		
4	egg whites	4
1 cup	granulated sugar	250 mL
2/3 cup	toasted sliced almonds	150 mL

Filling		
2 cups	whipping (35%) cream	500 mL
2 tbsp	confectioner's (icing) sugar, sifted	25 mL
1 tsp	vanilla extract	5 mL
2 cups	fresh strawberries	500 mL

1. *Cake:* In a large mixer bowl, combine cake mix, egg yolks, water and oil. Beat on medium speed for 2 minutes. Remove 2 cups (500 mL) batter. Spread it in extra prepared round or square pan. Bake as directed and reserve for another use. Spread remaining batter evenly in prepared round pans.

2. *Topping:* In a small mixer bowl, beat egg whites until frothy. Gradually add sugar, beating to stiff peaks. Carefully spread meringue over batter in round pans, sealing meringue to edge of pan. Sprinkle almonds evenly on top. Bake 25 to 30 minutes or until crisp and golden. Meringue will puff during baking. Cool completely in pans on a wire rack. Carefully remove from pans. (See Tip, at left, for technique.)

3. *Filling:* Beat cream, confectioner's sugar and vanilla together until stiff peaks form.

4. *Assembly:* Place 1 cake layer meringue-side down on a serving plate. Spread cream on top. Reserve a few whole berries for top. Slice remaining berries in half and place over cream. Put second cake layer meringue-side up over berries. Garnish top with whole berries. Chill until serving. Store leftover cake in refrigerator.

Ribbon Torte

Preheat oven to 350° F (180° C)
Two 8-inch (1 L) or 9-inch (1.5 L) round cake pans, greased and floured

Serves 10 to 12

1	pkg (18.25 oz [515 g]) fudge marble cake mix	1
3	eggs	3
1 1/4 cups	water	300 mL
1/3 cup	vegetable oil	75 mL
	Chocolate PUDDING & CREAM FILLING (see recipe, page 177)	
	Shaved chocolate or chocolate curls (optional)	

You can make a plain and a chocolate cake layer from one marble cake mix.

TIP

Chill your bowl and beaters before whipping cream to get the best volume and nice stiff peaks.

VARIATION

Replace the chocolate pudding with vanilla.

1. *Cake:* In a large mixer bowl, combine large cake mix packet, eggs, water and oil. Beat on medium speed for 2 minutes. Spread half of batter (about 2 1/2 cups [625 mL]) into one pan. Blend contents of small cocoa packet from cake mix into remaining batter. Mix well and spread in remaining pan. Bake as directed on package. Cool 10 minutes in pans on a wire rack then remove layers and cool completely. With a long, sharp knife, cut each layer horizontally in half to make 4 layers.

2. *Assembly:* Prepare chocolate PUDDING & CREAM FILLING. Place 1 halved cake layer cut-side up on serving plate. Spread one-quarter of cream mixture on top. Repeat with remaining cake, alternating light and dark layers with cream mixture between layers and on top. Decorate with shaved chocolate or chocolate curls, if desired. Chill until serving. Store leftover cake in refrigerator.

Chocolate Raspberry Torte

Preheat oven to 350° F (180° C)
Two 9-inch (1.5 L) round cake pans, greased and floured

Serves 10 to 12

You can't go wrong with the combination of chocolate, whipped cream and fresh raspberries.

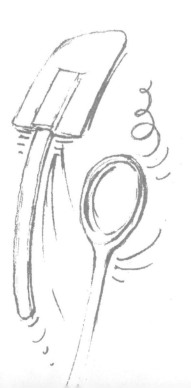

Cake		
1	pkg (18.25 oz [515 g]) devil's food or dark-chocolate cake mix	1
Filling		
2 cups	whipping (35%) cream	500 mL
1/4 cup	confectioner's (icing) sugar, sifted	50 mL
1 cup	raspberry jam	250 mL
Frosting		
1 1/2 cups	semi-sweet chocolate chips	375 mL
3/4 cup	sour cream	175 mL
	Chocolate curls	
	Fresh raspberries	

1. *Cake:* Prepare and bake cake according to package directions to make two 9-inch (23 cm) round cake layers. Cool 10 minutes in pans on a wire rack, then remove layers and cool completely. With a long, sharp knife, cut each layer horizontally in half to make 4 layers.

2. *Filling:* Beat whipping cream and confectioner's sugar until stiff peaks form.

3. *Frosting:* In top of a double boiler, melt chocolate chips or microwave on Medium for 2 minutes. Stir until smooth. Stir in sour cream.

4. *Assembly:* Place 1 halved cake layer cut-side up on a serving plate. Spread with 1/3 cup (75 mL) jam and one-third of the cream. Repeat layering, ending with top cake layer cut-side down. Frost top and sides of cake with frosting. Decorate with chocolate curls and fresh raspberries. Chill until serving. Store leftover cake in refrigerator.

Apricot Hazelnut Cake

Preheat oven to 350° F (180° C)
Two 8-inch (1.2 L) round cake pans, greased and floured

Serves 10 to 12

A feathery light, nutty, not-too-sweet delight. Simple but attractive.

VARIATION

Try using pecans in place of hazelnuts.

Cake

1	pkg (18.25 oz [515 g]) white cake mix	1
1 cup	ground hazelnuts	250 mL
4	eggs	4
1 1/3 cups	water	325 mL
1/3 cup	vegetable oil	75 mL
	APRICOT WHIPPED CREAM FILLING (see recipe, page 176)	

Glaze

| 1/2 cup | strained apricot jam | 125 mL |
| 1/4 cup | coarsely chopped hazelnuts (optional) | 50 mL |

1. *Cake:* In a large mixer bowl, combine cake mix, ground hazelnuts, eggs, water and oil. Beat on medium speed for 2 minutes. Spread batter in prepared pans, dividing evenly. Bake 30 to 35 minutes or until a toothpick inserted in center comes out clean. Cool 10 minutes in pans on a wire rack then remove layers and cool completely. With a long, sharp knife, cut each layer horizontally in half to make 4 layers.

2. *Assembly:* Prepare APRICOT WHIPPED CREAM FILLING. Place 1 halved cake layer on a serving plate. Spread with one-third of filling. Repeat with remaining 3 cake layers and filling, placing last cake layer top-side up.

3. *Glaze:* Warm jam if necessary to soften to a spreading consistency. Spread over top of cake, taking it right to the edge. Garnish, if desired, with a ring of chopped nuts. Chill until serving. Store leftover cake in refrigerator.

Banana Spice Cake with Cinnamon Banana Frosting

Preheat oven to 350° F (180° C)
Two 9-inch (1.5 L) round cake pans, greased and floured

Serves 10 to 12

The subtle spices in this cake help to bring out the banana flavor.

1	pkg (18.25 oz [515 g]) white cake mix	1
1/3 cup	packed brown sugar	75 mL
1 tsp	ground cinnamon	5 mL
1/4 tsp	ground nutmeg	1 mL
3	eggs	3
1 cup	water	250 mL
1 cup	mashed ripe bananas (2 or 3 bananas)	250 mL
1/2 cup	vegetable oil	125 mL
	BANANA BUTTER FROSTING (see recipe, page 163)	
1/4 tsp	ground cinnamon	1 mL

TIP

I like to mash bananas by hand using a fork on a flat plate. If you use a food processor, stop while the mixture is still thick. Don't overprocess or the texture of the bananas will become too thin.

VARIATION

This cake is also delicious with a cream cheese frosting flavored with a hint of cinnamon.

1. *Cake:* In a large mixer bowl, combine cake mix, brown sugar, 1 tsp (5 mL) cinnamon, nutmeg, eggs, water, mashed bananas and oil. Beat on medium speed for 2 minutes, or until smooth. Spread batter in prepared pans, dividing evenly. Bake 30 to 35 minutes or until a toothpick inserted in center comes out clean. Cool 10 minutes in pans on a wire rack, then remove layers and cool completely.

2. *Frosting:* Prepare BANANA BUTTER FROSTING, adding 1/4 tsp (5 mL) cinnamon with the confectioner's sugar.

3. *Assembly:* Place 1 cake layer top-side down on a serving plate. Spread a generous amount of frosting on top. Place second cake layer top-side up over frosting. Cover top and sides of cake with remaining frosting. Chill until serving and to firm up frosting for neater slicing.

Lemon Poppy Seed Layer Cake

Preheat oven to 350° F (180° C)
Two 9-inch (1.5 L) round cake pans, greased and floured

Serves 10 to 12

Poppy seeds add a pleasant crunch to this light, tangy, lemon-lover's cake. It's my mother's favorite cake, although she prefers it without the poppy seeds.

Cake

1	pkg (18.25 oz [515 g]) lemon cake mix	1
3	eggs	3
1 1/3 cups	water	325 mL
1/3 cup	vegetable oil	75 mL
1/4 cup	poppy seeds	50 mL

Lemon Curd Filling

2	eggs	2
6 tbsp	fresh lemon juice	90 mL
2 tbsp	grated lemon zest	25 mL
1 cup	granulated sugar	250 mL
1/4 cup	butter, softened	50 mL

Lemon BUTTER FROSTING (see recipe, page 161)

Candied lemon slices to garnish (optional)

1. *Cake:* In a large mixer bowl, combine cake mix, eggs, water and oil. Beat on medium speed for 2 minutes. Stir in poppy seeds. Spread batter in prepared pans, dividing evenly. Bake 30 to 35 minutes or until a toothpick inserted in center comes out clean. Cool 10 minutes in pans on a wire rack, then remove layers and cool completely. With a long, sharp knife, cut each layer horizontally in half to make 4 layers.

2. *Filling:* In a small saucepan, beat eggs, lemon juice, zest and sugar together to blend. Add butter. Cook over low heat, stirring constantly, until smoothly thickened. Remove from heat. Cover surface with plastic wrap and cool completely. Store in covered container in refrigerator.

3. *Assembly:* Prepare LEMON BUTTER FROSTING. Place top half of 1 cake layer cut-side up on a serving plate. Spread half of lemon filling over surface. Place bottom half of cake layer cut-side down on filling. Spread lemon frosting on center layer. Top with bottom half of remaining cake layer cut side up. Cover with remaining filling and put remaining top cake layer in place over filling. Cover top and sides of cake with remaining frosting. If desired, decorate with candied lemon slices. Chill overnight for optimum flavor and easy slicing.

Peaches 'n' Cream Cake

Serves 10 to 12

Not only does the peach gelatin add a whop of flavor to this cake but the color is unique too.

TIP

To keep layer cakes from slipping on your serving plate, spread a little frosting on the plate before putting the first cake layer down. This "glues" it to the plate.

For this frosting, use blocks of cream cheese at room temperature not the tubs of spreadable cream cheese.

VARIATION

Replace peaches with apricots. The flavor will be more intense than peach.

Preheat oven to 350° F (180° C)
Two 9-inch (1.5 L) round cake pans, greased and floured

1	can (28 oz [796 mL]) peach slices, well drained	1
1	pkg (18.25 oz [515 g]) white cake mix	1
1	pkg (3 oz [85 g]) peach-flavored gelatin dessert mix	1
4	eggs	4
1/3 cup	vegetable oil	75 mL
	Peach CREAM CHEESE FROSTING (see recipe, page 170)	

1. *Cake:* In a food processor, purée peaches. You should have about 2 cups (500 mL) of purée. Measure 1 1/4 cups (300 mL) purée for cake and 1/2 cup (125 mL) for frosting. In a large mixer bowl, combine cake mix, gelatin, eggs, peach purée and oil. Beat on medium speed for 2 minutes. Spread batter in prepared pans, dividing evenly. Bake 30 to 35 minutes or until a toothpick inserted in center comes out clean. Cool 10 minutes in pans on a wire rack, then remove layers and cool completely. With a long, sharp knife, cut each layer horizontally in half to make 4 layers.

2. *Assembly:* Prepare peach CREAM CHEESE FROSTING. Place 1 halved cake layer top-side down on a serving plate. Spread with about 1/3 cup (75 mL) frosting. Place bottom halved cake layer over frosting. Repeat layering of frosting and cake, placing last cake layer top-side up. Cover top and sides of cake with remaining frosting. Chill until serving. Store leftover cake in refrigerator.

Raspberry Dream Cake

Preheat oven to 350° F (180° C)
Two 9-inch (1.5 L) round cake pans, greased and floured

Serves 10 to12

*An adult raspberry taste
with a kid's color appeal.*

TIP

Always use large eggs in baking
unless otherwise specified.

Have all ingredients for cakes at
room temperature.

This cake freezes well without
the raspberry garnish.

VARIATION

Replace raspberry with
strawberry in both the cake
and frosting.

1	pkg (18.25 oz [515 g]) white cake mix	1
1	pkg (3 oz[85 g]) raspberry gelatin dessert mix	1
4	eggs	4
1 1/4 cups	plain or raspberry yogurt	300 mL
1/3 cup	vegetable oil	75 mL
	Raspberry BUTTER FROSTING (see recipe, page 161)	
	Fresh raspberries to garnish	

1. *Cake:* In a large mixer bowl, combine cake mix, gelatin, eggs, yogurt and oil. Beat on medium speed for 2 minutes. Spread batter in prepared pans, dividing evenly. Bake 30 to 35 minutes or until a toothpick inserted in center comes out clean. Cool 10 minutes in pans on a wire rack then remove layers and cool completely. With a long, sharp knife, cut each layer horizontally in half to make 4 layers.

2. *Assembly:* Prepare RASPBERRY BUTTER FROSTING. Place 1 halved cake layer top-side down on a serving plate. Spread with one-quarter of frosting. Place bottom halved cake layer over frosting. Repeat layering with remaining frosting and cake, ending with frosting on top. Decorate top with whole raspberries. Chill until serving.

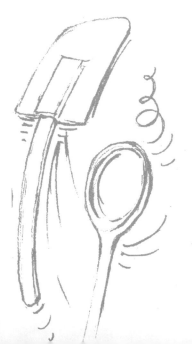

Black Forest Cake

Preheat oven to 350° F (180° C)
Three 8-inch (1.2 L) or 9-inch (1.5 L) round cake pans, greased and floured

Serves 10 to 12

A shortcut version of an all-time favorite, special-occasion cake.

The sour cherries in this recipe give a tart cherry filling. For a sweeter taste, a can of prepared cherry pie filling is quick and easy.

Maraschino cherries with stems can add a colorful touch on top of the cake.

Replace the chocolate pudding with vanilla.

Cake

1	pkg (18.25 oz [515 g]) devil's food cake mix	1

Cherry Filling

3 tbsp	granulated sugar	45 mL
3 tbsp	cornstarch	45 mL
28 oz	pitted sour cherries in syrup, well-drained, juice reserved	796 mL
1 1/4 cups	reserved cherry juice, plus water as necessary	300 mL

Whipped Cream Filling & Topping

3 cups	whipping (35%) cream	750 mL
1/2 cup	confectioner's (icing) sugar, sifted	125 mL
1/3 cup	cherry liqueur	75 mL
	Chocolate curls	

1. *Cake:* Prepare cake mix as directed on package. Spread batter in prepared pans, dividing evenly. Bake 20 to 25 minutes or until a toothpick inserted in center comes out clean. Cool 10 minutes in pans on a wire rack, then remove layers and cool completely.

2. *Cherry Filling:* In a saucepan mix sugar and cornstarch. Stir in cherry juice. Cook over medium heat, stirring constantly, until mixture comes to a boil thickens. Add cherries; cook for 1 minute longer. Cool completely.

3. *Whipped Cream Filling & Topping:* Beat whipping cream and confectioner's sugar to stiff peaks.

4. *Assembly:* If top of cakes is too rounded, trim to even off. Sprinkle each layer with liqueur. Place 1 cake layer on a serving plate. Spread half of cherry filling and one-quarter of cream over cake. Add middle cake layer. Spread with remaining cherries and one-quarter of cream. Add top cake layer. Cover top and sides of cake with remaining cream. Decorate with chocolate curls. Chill at least 2 hours to allow flavors to mellow. Store leftover cake in refrigerator.

Double Chocolate Cake

Preheat oven to 350° F (180° C)
Two 9-inch (1.5 L) round cake pans, greased and floured

Serves 10 to 12

A chocolate cake made more chocolatey with the addition of cocoa.

1	pkg (18.25 oz [515 g]) devil's food cake mix	1
1/4 cup	cocoa powder	50 mL
4	eggs	4
1 1/2 cups	plain yogurt	375 mL
1/2 cup	vegetable oil	125 mL

WHITE CHOCOLATE CREAM CHEESE FROSTING (see recipe, page 171)

Chocolate curls or shaved chocolate (optional)

(see recipe, page 171)

TIP

Cocoa powder tends to clump in storage. Sift it before adding it to other dry ingredients to be sure the lumps disappear in mixing.

When melting chocolate use squares rather than chips. Chips are formulated to keep their shape during baking so they don't melt as smoothly as squares.

VARIATION

Add 1 tsp (5 mL) almond extract or 1 tbsp (15 mL) instant coffee powder to cake batter.

---

1. *Cake:* In a large mixer bowl, combine cake mix, cocoa, eggs, yogurt and oil. Beat on medium speed for 2 minutes, or until smooth. Spread batter in prepared pans, dividing evenly. Bake 30 to 35 minutes or until a toothpick inserted in center comes out clean. Cool 10 minutes in pans on a wire rack then remove layers and cool completely.

2. *Assembly:* Prepare WHITE CHOCOLATE CREAM CHEESE FROSTING. Place 1 cake layer top-side down on a serving plate. Spread with a generous amount of frosting. Place second cake layer top-side up over frosting. Cover top and sides of cake with remaining frosting. Decorate with chocolate curls, if desired. Chill until serving.

Carrot Cake with Orange Cream Cheese Frosting

Preheat oven to 350° F (180° C)
Two 9-inch (1.5 L) round cake pans, greased and floured

Serves 10 to 12

Orange adds a nice touch to the traditional mildly spiced carrot cake and plain cream cheese frosting.

Peel carrots before grating to prevent them turning green in the baked cake.

1	pkg (18.25 oz [515 g]) white cake mix	1
1	pkg (4-serving size) vanilla instant pudding mix	1
1 1/2 tsp	ground cinnamon	7 mL
1/4 tsp	ground nutmeg	1 mL
4	eggs	4
3/4 cup	orange juice	175 mL
1/2 cup	vegetable oil	125 mL
3 cups	peeled, grated carrots	750 mL
3/4 cup	raisins	175 mL
1 tbsp	grated orange zest	15 mL

Orange CREAM CHEESE FROSTING
(see recipe, page 170)

1. *Cake:* In a large mixer bowl, combine cake mix, pudding mix, spices, eggs, orange juice and oil. Beat on medium speed for 2 minutes or until smooth. Add carrots, raisins and zest. Mix well. Spread batter in prepared pans, dividing evenly. Bake 35 to 40 minutes or until a toothpick inserted in center comes out clean. Cool 10 minutes in pans on a wire rack then remove layers and cool completely.

2. *Assembly:* Prepare orange CREAM CHEESE FROSTING. Place 1 cake layer top-side down on a serving plate. Spread a generous amount of frosting on top. Place second cake layer top-side up over frosting. Cover top and sides of cake with remaining frosting. Chill until serving.

Twin Boston Cream Pies

Preheat oven to 350° F (180° C)
Two 9-inch (1.5 L) round cake pans, greased and floured

Serves 12 to 16

A good choice for a crowd, since this recipe makes two cakes.

TIP

Don't be confused by the name of this recipe. Although called a "pie", it's really a cake with a vanilla custard filling and chocolate glaze.

VARIATION

Although not traditional, a chocolate filling is also nice. Replace the vanilla pudding mix with a chocolate one.

Cake

1	pkg (18.25 oz [515 g]) yellow cake mix	1

Filling

1	pkg (4-serving size) vanilla instant pudding mix	1
1 1/4 cups	milk	300 mL

Chocolate Glaze

1 cup	ready-to-serve chocolate frosting	250 mL

1. *Cake:* Prepare and bake cake according to package directions for two 9-inch (23 cm) layers. Cool 10 minutes in pans on a wire rack then remove layers and cool completely. With a long, sharp knife, cut each layer horizontally in half to make 4 layers.

2. *Filling:* In a small bowl, combine pudding mix and milk. Beat on low speed for 1 minute. Let stand 5 minutes to set.

3. *Assembly:* You'll need 2 serving plates. Place bottom cake layers on plates. Spread half of filling on each layer. Place top cake layers over filling.

4. *Glaze:* In a microwave on High , heat frosting in a microwaveable container for 30 to 40 seconds, or set frosting container in a pot of hot water to soften to a shiny, thick pouring consistency. Pour over top of cakes to cover completely and let some drizzle down the sides. Chill to set chocolate glaze. Store leftover cake in refrigerator.

Apricot Cream Cake

Preheat oven to 350° F (180° C)
Two 9-inch (1.5 L) round cake pans, greased and floured

Serves 10 to 12

2	cans (each 14 oz [398 mL]) apricot halves, drained, 1/2 cup [125 mL] syrup reserved	2
1	pkg (18.25 oz [515 g]) white cake mix	1
4	eggs	4
1/2 cup	butter, melted	125 mL

APRICOT WHIPPED CREAM FILLING
(see recipe, page 176)

Canned apricots have a wonderful flavor and give a summery taste to an all-year-round cake.

(see recipe, page 176)

1. *Cake:* Reserve 4 apricot halves for garnish. In a food processor, purée apricots to make 1 1/2 cups (375 mL) purée. In a large mixer bowl, combine cake mix, eggs, apricot purée and melted butter. Beat at medium speed for 2 minutes. Spread batter in prepared pans, dividing evenly. Bake 30 to 35 minutes or until a toothpick inserted in center comes out clean. Cool 10 minutes in pans on a wire rack, then remove layers and place right-side up on rack over waxed paper. Poke holes in top of warm cakes with a fork or toothpick. Brush reserved apricot syrup over cakes using 1/4 cup (50 mL) for each layer, letting it soak in. Cool completely. With a long, sharp knife, cut each layer horizontally in half to make 4 layers.

2. *Assembly:* Prepare APRICOT WHIPPED CREAM FILLING. Place 1 halved cake layer on a serving plate. Spread with one-quarter of filling. Repeat layering with remaining cake and filling. Slice reserved apricot halves and arrange on top of cake. Chill until serving. Store leftover cake in refrigerator.

TIP

A food processor is the best way to purée the apricots. But if you don't have one, a potato masher also works well.

A garnish of mint leaves is attractive.

VARIATION

Replace apricots with peaches.

TUBE & BUNDT CAKES

Orange Angel Cream Cake

Preheat oven to 325° F (160° C)
10-inch (4 L) tube pan, ungreased

Serves 12 to 16

Refreshingly light and creamy, is easy to enjoy – this cake even after a hearty meal.

TIP

Prepare cake ahead, keeping last-minute preparation for your dinner to a minimum.

VARIATION

Replace orange zest with lemon zest and half the juice with lemon juice.

Cake

1	pkg (16 oz [450 g]) white angel food cake mix	1
1 cup	water	250 mL
1/3 cup	orange juice	75 mL
1 tbsp	grated orange zest	15 mL
2 or 3	drops orange or yellow food coloring (optional)	2 or 3

Orange Cream Filling & Topping

2 cups	whipping (35%) cream	500 mL
2 tbsp	confectioner's (icing) sugar, sifted	25 mL
2 tsp	grated orange zest	10 mL
	Mandarin orange segments (optional)	

1. *Cake:* In a large mixer bowl, combine cake mix, water, orange juice, zest and, if using, food coloring. Beat on low speed for 30 seconds, then on medium speed for 1 minute. Pour into ungreased pan. Bake according to package directions. With an electric knife or a long, sharp, serrated knife, cut cake horizontally to make 3 layers.

2. *Filling & Topping:* Beat whipping cream and confectioner's sugar to stiff peaks. Fold in zest. Spread cream between layers and on top of cake. Garnish with mandarins, if desired. Chill until serving. Store leftover cake in refrigerator.

Double Chocolate Rum Cake

Preheat oven to 350° F (180° C)
10-inch (4 L) tube pan, greased and floured

Serves 12 to 16

A dense, moist chocolate cake layered with a creamy chocolate rum filling. A nice and easy dessert for entertaining.

TIP

All recipes in this book were tested using large eggs. One large egg measures 1/4 cup (50 mL). If you're using a different size, break eggs into a measuring cup to get the correct 1 cup (250 mL) measure.

You can use rum extract in place of real rum. For the cake, mix 1 tbsp (15 mL) rum extract and 1/4 cup (50 mL) water. For the filling, mix 1 1/2 tsp (7 mL) extract and 3 tbsp (45 mL) water.

VARIATION

Replace chocolate pudding with vanilla for a milder chocolate flavor.

Cake

1	pkg (18.25 oz [515 g]) chocolate cake mix	1
1	pkg (4-serving size) chocolate instant pudding mix	1
4	eggs	4
2/3 cup	water	150 mL
1/2 cup	vegetable oil	125 mL
1/3 cup	rum	75 mL

Chocolate Rum Filling

1	envelope (1.3 oz [42.5 g]) dessert topping mix	1
1	pkg (4-serving size) chocolate instant pudding mix	1
1 cup	cold milk	250 mL
1/4 cup	rum	50 mL
	Confectioner's (icing) sugar (optional)	

1. *Cake:* In a large mixer bowl, combine cake mix, pudding mix, eggs, water, oil and rum. Beat on medium speed for 2 minutes. Spread batter evenly in prepared pan. Bake 55 to 60 minutes or until a cake tester inserted in center comes out clean. Cool 25 minutes in pan on a wire rack, then remove cake and cool completely. With a long, sharp knife, cut cake horizontally to make 3 layers.

2. *Filling:* In a small mixer bowl, combine topping mix, pudding mix, milk and rum. Beat on high speed for about 7 minutes or until fluffy. Place bottom cake layer on a serving plate. Spread half of cream mixture on top. Place middle cake layer over the cream and spread with remaining cream. Put top cake layer in place. Chill until serving. Finish with a dusting of confectioner's sugar before serving, if desired. Store leftover cake in refrigerator.

Piña Colada Cake

Preheat oven to 350° F (180° C)
10-inch (3 L) Bundt or (4 L) tube pan, greased and floured

Serves 12 to 16

A favorite drink is also a favorite cake. It's hard to beat the flavor of a blend of pineapple, coconut and rum.

TIP

Coconut milk sold in a can is different from coconut cream, which is a solid.

Whatever rum you prefer – light, dark or amber – is fine.

Dried pineapple chunks are a nice garnish and keep well.

Cake

1	pkg (18.25 oz [515 g]) white cake mix	1
1	pkg (4-serving size) vanilla instant pudding mix	1
4	eggs	4
1/2 cup	coconut milk	125 mL
1/3 cup	rum	75 mL
1/3 cup	vegetable oil	75 mL
2/3 cup	well-drained crushed pineapple	150 mL

Coconut Glaze

3/4 cup	coconut milk	175 mL
2 tbsp	rum	25 mL

1. *Cake:* In a large mixer bowl, combine cake mix, pudding mix, eggs, coconut milk, rum and oil. Beat on medium speed for 2 minutes. Stir in crushed pineapple. Spread batter evenly in prepared pan. Bake 45 to 55 minutes or until a cake tester inserted in center comes out clean. Cool 20 minutes in pan on a wire rack, then remove cake and invert onto wire rack over waxed paper.

2. *Glaze:* Combine coconut milk and rum. Poke holes in warm cake with a fork or a toothpick. Brush glaze over cake, letting it soak in. Cool completely before cutting.

Hummingbird Cake

Preheat oven to 350° F (180° C)
10-inch (3 L) Bundt or (4 L) tube pan, greased and floured

Serves 12 to 16

The name of this recipe has been around for years, and there are many different versions, except that they all contain pineapple and banana.

TIP

Mashed bananas not only add flavor to cakes but keep them moist. The pudding mix adds sweetness and gives a hearty but tender texture to a mix.

A dusting of confectioner's sugar before serving (or a white icing drizzle) finishes off this cake beautifully.

VARIATION

Use banana cream instant pudding for a more pronounced banana flavor.

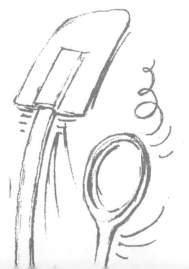

1	pkg (18.25 oz [515 g]) white cake mix	1
1	pkg (4-serving size) vanilla instant pudding mix	1
4	eggs	4
2/3 cup	well-drained crushed pineapple, juice reserved	150 mL
1 cup	reserved pineapple juice (see above), plus water as necessary	250 mL
1/2 cup	vegetable oil	125 mL
1 tsp	ground cinnamon	5 mL
1/2 cup	finely chopped pecans	125 mL
Half	medium-size ripe banana, diced	Half
1/3 cup	chopped maraschino cherries	75 mL

1. *Cake:* In a large mixer bowl, combine cake mix, pudding mix, eggs, drained pineapple, pineapple juice, oil and cinnamon. Beat on low speed for 1 minute to blend, then on medium speed for 2 minutes. Stir in pecans, banana and cherries. Spread evenly in prepared pan. Bake 45 to 55 minutes or until a cake tester inserted in center comes out clean. Cool 25 minutes in pan on a wire rack then remove cake and cool completely. Dust with confectioner's sugar or drizzle with a vanilla glaze, if desired.

Orange Chiffon Cake

Preheat oven to 325° F (160° C)
10-inch (4 L) tube pan, ungreased

Serves 12 to 16

Feathery light and not too sweet. It's nice with a thin orange glaze or fresh fruit.

Cake

5	egg whites	5
1/2 tsp	cream of tartar	2 mL
1	pkg (18.25 oz [515 g]) white cake mix	1
3	egg yolks	3
1/2 cup	frozen orange juice concentrate, thawed	125 mL
1/2 cup	water	125 mL
1/2 cup	vegetable oil	125 mL

Orange Glaze

2 cups	confectioner's (icing) sugar, sifted	500 mL
3 tbsp	orange juice	45 mL

1. *Cake:* In a small mixer bowl on high speed, beat egg whites and cream of tartar until stiff peaks form. Set aside. In a large mixer bowl, combine cake mix, egg yolks, orange juice concentrate, water and oil. Beat on medium speed for 2 minutes. Fold egg whites into batter gently but thoroughly. Pour batter carefully into ungreased pan. Bake 45 to 55 minutes or until a cake tester inserted in center comes out clean. Remove pan from oven and immediately turn upside down, placing center tube of pan on an upside-down glass or cup. Cool 1 hour. Run a long, sharp knife around edge of pan and center ring to loosen cake. Remove cake. Place right-side up on wire rack to cool completely.

2. *Glaze:* Stir together confectioner's sugar and enough orange juice to create a soft, smooth consistency. Spread over top and sides of cake. Leave 30 minutes to let glaze set before cutting.

CHOCOLATE RASPBERRY TORTE (PAGE 47) ➤
OVERLEAF: CHOO CHOO TRAIN BIRTHDAY CAKE (PAGE 103)

Tequila Orange Sunrise

Preheat oven to 350° F (180° C)
10-inch (3 L) Bundt or (4 L) tube pan, greased and floured

Serves 12 to 16

A popular drink in edible form.

TIP

You can replace the orange juice concentrate and water with 3/4 cup (175 mL) orange juice, but the flavor will be milder.

The alcohol bakes out, so don't worry about driving after you eat this dessert!

If you prefer, a dusting of confectioner's sugar can replace the glaze.

VARIATION

Replace tequila with an orange or peach liqueur.

Cake

1	pkg (18.25 oz [515 g]) white cake mix	1
1	pkg (4-serving size) vanilla instant pudding mix	1
4	eggs	4
1/2 cup	tequila	125 mL
1/2 cup	water	125 mL
1/2 cup	vegetable oil	125 mL
1/4 cup	frozen orange juice concentrate, thawed	50 mL

Orange Glaze

1 cup	confectioner's (icing) sugar, sifted	250 mL
1 tbsp	frozen orange juice concentrate, thawed	15 mL

1. *Cake:* In a large mixer bowl, combine cake mix, pudding mix, eggs, tequila, water, oil and orange juice concentrate. Beat for 2 minutes on medium speed. Spread batter evenly in prepared pan. Bake 45 to 50 minutes or until a cake tester inserted in center comes out clean. Cool 25 minutes in pan on wire rack, then remove cake and cool completely.

2. *Glaze:* Combine confectioner's sugar and orange juice concentrate, mixing until smooth. Add a little more confectioner's sugar or liquid if necessary to make a thick pouring consistency. Drizzle over cooled cake.

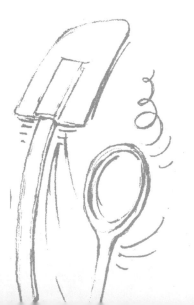

◄ DECADENT CHOCOLATE BUNDT CAKE (PAGE 75)

Chocolate Macaroon Ring Cake

Preheat oven to 350° F (180° C)
10-inch (4 L) tube pan, greased and floured

Serves 12 to 16

The macaroon filling sinks during baking to produce an attractive white swirl through the center of the chocolate cake.

Filling		
2	egg whites	2
1/2 tsp	almond extract	2 mL
1/2 cup	granulated sugar	125 mL
1/2 cup	flaked coconut	125 mL
1/4 cup	all-purpose flour	50 mL
Cake		
1	pkg (18.25 oz [515 g]) devil's food cake mix	1
2	egg yolks	2
1	egg	1
1 cup	water	250 mL
1/3 cup	vegetable oil	75 mL
Glaze		
1 cup	confectioner's (icing) sugar, sifted	250 mL
4 tsp	milk	20 mL
1 tsp	vegetable oil	5 mL

1. *Filling:* In a small mixer bowl on high speed, beat egg whites and almond extract until frothy. Gradually add sugar, beating to soft peaks. Stir in coconut and flour, mixing gently but thoroughly.

2. *Cake:* In a large mixer bowl, combine cake mix, egg yolks, whole egg, water and oil. Beat on medium speed for 2 minutes. Pour half of batter into prepared pan. Spoon filling over batter without allowing it to touch sides of pan. Cover with remaining batter. Bake 55 to 65 minutes or until a cake tester inserted in center comes out clean. Cool 25 minutes in pan on a wire rack, then remove cake and cool completely.

3. *Glaze:* Combine all glaze ingredients, adding enough milk to make a smooth consistency. Spread glaze over top of cake, letting it drip down the sides.

Chocolate Pineapple Carrot Cake

Preheat oven to 350° F (180° C)
10-inch (3 L) Bundt pan, greased and floured

Serves 12 to 16

A decadent twist on an all-time favorite.

TIP

Brands of crushed pineapple vary considerably. Choose one that has coarse rather than fine pineapple pieces and not too much liquid.

VARIATION

Replace grated carrot with zucchini.

1	pkg (18.25 oz [515 g]) devil's food cake mix	1
2 tsp	ground cinnamon	10 mL
1/4 tsp	ground nutmeg	1 mL
3	eggs	3
1/2 cup	vegetable oil	125 mL
1 cup	crushed pineapple, with juice	250 mL
1/4 cup	water	50 mL
2 cups	grated peeled carrots	500 mL
	CHOCOLATE CREAM CHEESE FROSTING (see recipe, page 172)	

1. *Cake:* In a large mixer bowl, combine cake mix, spices, eggs, oil, pineapple, water and carrots. Beat on low speed for 1 minute to blend, then on medium speed for 2 minutes. Spread in prepared pan. Bake 45 to 55 minutes or until a cake tester inserted in center comes out clean. Cool 25 minutes in pan on a wire rack, then remove cake and cool completely.

2. Prepare CHOCOLATE CREAM CHEESE FROSTING. Spread on top of cake.

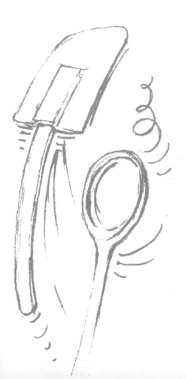

Peach and Blueberry Pudding Cake

Preheat oven to 350° F (180° C)
10-inch (3 L) Bundt pan, greased and floured

Serves 12 to 16

An easy-to-make cake that tastes as good as it looks. It's nice plain or with whipped cream for special occasions.

1	pkg (18.25 oz [515 g]) white cake mix	1
1	pkg (4-serving size) vanilla instant pudding mix	1
4	eggs	4
1/2 cup	sour cream	125 mL
1/4 cup	vegetable oil	50 mL
1 cup	diced peaches	250 mL
1 cup	blueberries	250 mL

TIP

If using fresh peaches that are very juicy, decrease sour cream to 1/3 cup (75 mL).

VARIATION

Replace blueberries with raspberries.

1. In a large mixer bowl, combine cake mix, pudding mix, eggs, sour cream and oil. Beat on low speed for 1 minute to blend, then on medium speed for 2 minutes. Fold in peaches and blueberries gently but thoroughly. Spread batter evenly in prepared pan. Bake 55 to 60 minutes or until a cake tester inserted in center comes out clean. Cool 25 minutes in pan on a wire rack, then remove cake and cool completely.

Cranberry Almond Lemon Cake

Preheat oven to 350° F (180° C)
10-inch (4 L) tube pan, greased and floured

Serves 12 to 16

Don't limit this wonderful cake to the traditional cranberry season. Keep a bag of frozen berries on hand to enjoy it year round.

1	pkg (18.25 oz [515 g]) white cake mix	1
1	pkg (4-serving size) lemon instant pudding mix	1
4	eggs	4
1 1/3 cups	sour cream	325 mL
1/2 cup	vegetable oil	125 mL
1/2 tsp	ground nutmeg	2 mL
1 1/4 cups	fresh cranberries *or* frozen, thawed (see Tip, at left)	300 mL
3/4 cup	sliced almonds	75 mL
	Confectioner's (icing) sugar for dusting (optional)	

TIP

If using frozen cranberries, thaw and pat dry before folding into batter.

VARIATION

For an interesting color, use unblanched almonds.

Replace cranberries with blueberries.

1. In a large mixer bowl, combine cake mix, pudding mix, eggs, sour cream, oil and nutmeg. Beat on medium speed for 2 minutes. Fold in cranberries and almonds. Spread batter in prepared pan. Bake 45 to 55 minutes or until a cake tester inserted in center comes out clean. Cool 25 minutes in pan on a wire rack, then remove cake and cool completely. Dust with confectioner's sugar before serving, if desired.

Pineapple Banana Cake

Preheat oven to 350° F (180° C)
10-inch (4 L) tube pan, greased and floured

Serves 12 to 16

A quick-to-make, moist tropical cake.

Cake

1	pkg (18.25 oz [515 g]) white cake mix	1
3	eggs	3
1 1/2 cups	mashed bananas (3 or 4 large bananas)	375 mL
1/2 cup	well-drained crushed pineapple	125 mL
1/3 cup	vegetable oil	75 mL
1 cup	chopped walnuts (optional)	250 mL

Pineapple Butter Frosting (optional)

1/4 cup	butter, softened	50 mL
1/3 cup	well-drained crushed pineapple, juice reserved	75 mL
3 cups	confectioner's (icing) sugar, sifted	750 mL
2 to 3 tbsp	reserved pineapple juice	25 to 45 mL

1. *Cake:* In a large mixer bowl, combine cake mix, eggs, mashed bananas, pineapple and oil. Beat on medium speed for 2 minutes. Stir in nuts. Spread batter in prepared pan. Bake 55 to 65 minutes or until a cake tester inserted in center comes out clean. Cool 25 minutes in pan on a wire rack, then remove cake and cool completely.

2. *Frosting:* Beat butter and pineapple together until smooth. Gradually add confectioner's sugar and pineapple juice, beating to a soft spreading consistency. Spread over cooled cake.

Hazelnut Rum Cake

Preheat oven to 350° F (180° C)
10-inch (3 L) Bundt or (4 L) tube pan, greased and floured

Serves 12 to 16

A novel way to enjoy your cocktail.

Cake

1	pkg (18.25 oz [515 g]) yellow cake mix	1
1	pkg (4-serving size) vanilla instant pudding mix	1
4	eggs	4
2/3 cup	water	150 mL
1/2 cup	vegetable oil	125 mL
1/3 cup	rum	75 mL
3/4 cup	chopped hazelnuts	175 mL

Glaze

1/3 cup	butter	75 mL
2 tbsp	water	25 mL
2/3 cup	granulated sugar	150 mL
1/3 cup	rum	75 mL

1. *Cake:* In a large mixer bowl, combine cake mix, pudding mix, eggs, water, oil and rum. Beat on medium speed for 2 minutes. Stir in nuts. Spread batter evenly in prepared pan. Bake 55 to 65 minutes or until a cake tester inserted in center comes out clean. Cool 20 minutes in pan on a wire rack, then remove cake and place on rack over waxed paper.

2. *Glaze:* In a small saucepan, melt butter. Add water and sugar. Bring mixture to a boil over medium heat, then simmer for 5 minutes, stirring constantly, until thickened. Remove from heat. Stir in rum. Poke holes over surface of warm cake with a fork or a toothpick. Brush glaze over cake, letting it soak in. Cool completely before cutting.

Cherry Almond Cake

Preheat oven to 350° F (180° C)
10-inch (4 L) tube pan, greased and floured

Serves 12 to 16

1	pkg (18.25 oz [515 g]) white cake mix	1
1	pkg (4-serving size) vanilla instant pudding mix	1
4	eggs	4
1 cup	sour cream	250 mL
1/2 cup	vegetable oil	125 mL
2 cups	candied red cherries, halved	500 mL
2/3 cup	coarsely chopped blanched almonds	150 mL

A good alternative to the traditional holiday fruitcake. This festive cake is a colorful addition to any tray and makes a welcome gift for the hard-to-buy-for people.

1. *Cake:* In a large mixer bowl, combine cake mix, pudding mix, eggs, sour cream and oil. Beat on medium speed for 2 minutes. Stir in cherries and almonds gently but thoroughly. Spread batter evenly in prepared pan. Bake 50 to 60 minutes, or until cake tester inserted in center comes out clean. Cool 25 minutes in pan on a wire rack, then remove cake and cool completely. Store at least overnight to let flavors mellow. For longer storage, keep refrigerated and cut as needed.

TIP

Chill cake for easy slicing.

For gift giving, wrap cooled cake tightly in plastic wrap and store in refrigerator. Add a pretty bow, a gift tag and card with the recipe on it.

VARIATION

All red or all green cherries looks good, but a combination is attractive too.

Substitute candied pineapple for half the cherries.

Lemon Pistachio Cake

Preheat oven to 350° F (180° C)
10-inch (3 L) Bundt or (4 L) tube pan, greased and floured

Serves 12 to 16

1	pkg (18.25 oz [515 g]) lemon cake mix	1
1	pkg (3 oz [85 g]) lemon-flavored gelatin dessert mix	1
4	eggs	4
1 1/4 cups	water	300 mL
1/2 cup	vegetable oil	125 mL
3/4 cup	finely chopped pistachio nuts	175 mL
	LEMON GLAZE (see recipe, page 181) (optional)	

The combination may sound strange but this cake not only looks great, it tastes great too.
The lemon glaze isn't necessary, but it finishes the cake off nicely.

TIP

Measure confectioner's sugar, then sift it before mixing with other ingredients to ensure lumps are removed.

One medium lemon should yield about 3 tbsp (45 mL) juice.

1. *Cake:* In a large mixer bowl, combine cake mix, gelatin mix, eggs, water and oil. Beat on medium speed for 2 minutes. Stir in nuts. Spread batter evenly in prepared pan. Bake 50 to 60 minutes or until a cake tester inserted in center comes out clean. Cool 25 minutes in pan on a wire rack, then remove cake and cool completely. Drizzle with lemon glaze, if desired.

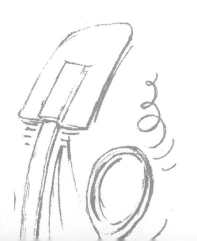

Spicy Zucchini Cake with Brown Sugar Fudge Frosting

Preheat oven to 350° F (180° C)
10-inch (4 L) tube pan, greased and floured

Serves 12 to 16

It's hard to decide which is best – the cake or the frosting.

Don't peel the zucchini – the skins are tender and the green fleck is interesting in the cake.

Use medium-size zucchini. The overgrown ones are seedy and quite wet.

The frosting hardens quickly on cooling, so use immediately after mixing. If necessary, rewarm on low heat to soften.

Substitute grated carrot for the zucchini.

Bake in 2 round pans for a layer cake and frost with CREAM CHEESE FROSTING (see recipe, page 170).

Cake

1	pkg (18.25 oz [515 g]) spice cake mix	1
1	pkg (4-serving size) vanilla instant pudding mix	1
4	eggs	4
1 cup	sour cream	250 mL
1/4 cup	vegetable oil	50 mL
2 1/2 cups	grated zucchini	625 mL
3/4 cup	chopped nuts	175 mL

Brown Sugar Fudge Frosting

1/2 cup	packed brown sugar	125 mL
1/4 cup	butter	50 mL
2 tbsp	light (10%) cream	25 mL
1 cup	confectioner's (icing) sugar, sifted	250 mL

1. *Cake:* In a large mixer bowl, combine cake mix, pudding mix, eggs, sour cream and oil. Beat on medium speed for 2 minutes. Stir in zucchini and nuts, mixing well. Spread batter evenly in prepared pan. Bake 60 to 65 minutes or until a cake tester inserted in center comes out clean. Cool 25 minutes in pan on a wire rack, then remove cake and cool completely.

2. *Frosting:* In a medium saucepan, combine brown sugar and butter. Bring to a boil over medium heat, then simmer for 2 minutes, stirring constantly. Carefully stir in cream. Return mixture to a boil, then remove from heat. Cool slightly. Put confectioner's sugar into a large mixer bowl. Pour warm brown sugar mixture on top. Beat on low speed just until smooth and creamy, about 2 minutes. Quickly spread on top and partially down sides of cake. Cool to let frosting set before cutting.

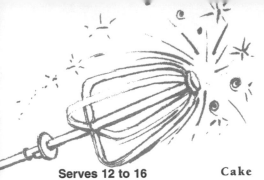

Decadent Chocolate Bundt Cake

Preheat oven to 350° F (180° C)
10-inch (3 L) Bundt pan, greased and floured

Serves 12 to 16

Easy, moist and loaded with chocolate. What could be better?

TIP

Whatever you put in a Bundt pan will look special. You can use a 13- by 9-inch (3.5 L) pan and bake about 40 minutes if you don't have a tube pan.

For a sweeter cake, use all of the chips for the cake and frost with a ready-to-serve chocolate frosting, warmed slightly for easy spreading.

VARIATION

Replace milk chocolate chips with semi-sweet or white.

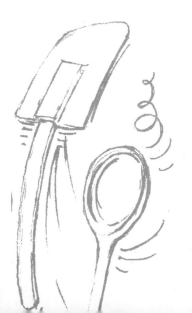

Cake

1	pkg (18.25 oz [515 g]) devil's food cake mix	1
1	pkg (4-serving size) chocolate instant pudding mix	1
4	eggs	4
1 cup	sour cream	250 mL
1/2 cup	water	125 mL
1 cup	milk chocolate chips	250 mL

Frosting

2/3 cup	milk chocolate chips, melted	150 mL
1/3 cup	sour cream	75 mL

1. *Cake:* In a large mixer bowl, combine cake mix, pudding mix, eggs, sour cream and water. Beat on medium speed for 2 minutes. Stir in chocolate chips. Spread batter evenly in prepared pan. Bake 50 to 60 minutes or until a cake tester inserted in center comes out clean. Cool 25 minutes in pan on a wire rack, then remove cake and cool completely.

2. *Frosting:* Combine melted chocolate chips and sour cream, stirring until smooth. Spread over top of cake. Cool to let frosting set.

Apple Cranberry Spice Cake

Preheat oven to 350° F (180° C)
10-inch (3 L) Bundt or (4 L) tube pan, greased and floured

Serves 12 to 16

*Cinnamon, apples and cran-
berries are a natural
combination in this cake.*

1	pkg (18.25 oz [515 g]) spice cake mix	1
3	eggs	3
1 cup	unsweetened applesauce	250 mL
1/2 cup	butter, softened	125 mL
1/4 cup	water	50 mL
1 cup	diced peeled apples	250 mL
1 cup	dried cranberries	250 mL

TIP

Spy, Spartan and Golden
Delicious are great apples
for baking.

VARIATION

Replace cranberries with dried
cherries or raisins.

1. In a large mixer bowl, combine cake mix, eggs, apple-
    sauce, butter and water. Beat on low speed for
    1 minute to blend, then on medium speed for 2 min-
    utes. Stir in diced apples and cranberries. Spread bat-
    ter evenly in prepared pan. Bake 55 to 65 minutes or
    until a cake tester inserted in center comes out clean.
    Cool 25 minutes in pan on a wire rack, then remove
    cake and cool completely.

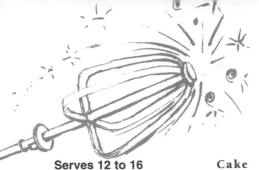

Apricot Almond Cake

Preheat oven to 350° F (180° C)
10-inch (3 L) Bundt or (4 L) tube pan, greased and floured

Serves 12 to 16

Apricot baby food gives great color and flavor to cakes with no work involved for the cook!

TIP

You can keep unfrosted cake in the refrigerator for about 5 days or about 3 months in the freezer.

You may want to double the topping. People always seem to want more than you plan on!

VARIATION

Replace apricot baby food with peach or plum.

Cake

1	pkg (18.25 oz [515 g]) white cake mix	1
4	eggs	4
1 cup	sour cream	250 mL
1 cup	apricot baby food	250 mL
1 cup	finely chopped almonds	250 mL

Apricot Cream Topping

1 cup	whipping (35%) cream	250 mL
2 tbsp	confectioner's (icing) sugar, sifted	25 mL
1/2 cup	apricot baby food	125 mL

1. *Cake:* In a large mixer bowl, combine cake mix, eggs, sour cream and baby food. Beat on low speed for 1 minute to blend, then on medium speed for 2 minutes. Fold in almonds. Spread batter evenly in prepared pan. Bake 40 to 50 minutes or until a cake tester inserted in center comes out clean. Cool 25 minutes in pan on a wire rack then remove cake and cool completely.

2. *Topping:* In a small bowl, beat cream and confectioner's sugar together until stiff peaks form. Fold in apricot baby food gently but thoroughly. Serve with slices of cake.

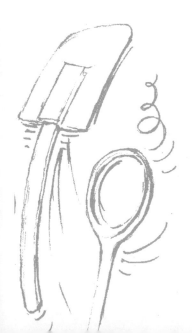

Hawaiian Dream Cake

Preheat oven to 350° F (180° C)
10-inch (4 L) tube pan, greased and floured

Serves 12 to 16

*The tropical taste will make
winter's long, cold nights
seem easier to endure.*

TIP

Toast coconut for a nutty flavor.
Spread out in a shallow pan and
bake at 350° F (180° C) for
about 10 minutes, stirring often
until golden. Cool completely.

VARIATION

Omit coconut if desired.

Cake

1	pkg (18.25 oz [515 g]) lemon cake mix	1
4	eggs	4
1 cup	crushed pineapple, with juice	250 mL
1/2 cup	vegetable oil	125 mL
1/2 cup	toasted flaked coconut	125 mL

Pineapple Cream Cheese Frosting

4 oz	cream cheese, softened	125 g
1/4 cup	butter, softened	50 mL
2 cups	confectioner's (icing) sugar, sifted	500 mL
3 tbsp	well-drained crushed pineapple	45 mL
	Toasted coconut (optional)	

1. *Cake:* In a large mixer bowl, combine cake mix, eggs, pineapple (with juice) and oil. Beat on medium speed for 2 minutes. Stir in coconut. Spread batter evenly in prepared pan. Bake 45 to 55 minutes or until a cake tester inserted in center comes out clean. Cool 25 minutes in pan on a wire rack, then remove cake and cool completely.

2. *Frosting:* In a large mixer bowl on medium speed, beat cream cheese and butter together to blend. Gradually add confectioner's sugar, beating until smooth and creamy. Fold in pineapple. Spread over cooled cake. Sprinkle with toasted coconut, if desired.

COFFEE CAKES

Chocolate Chip Coffee Cake

Preheat oven to 350° F (180° C)
13- by 9-inch (3.5 L) cake pan, greased

Serves 12 to 16

*A perfect coffee-time treat.
It freezes well, so keep a
piece on hand for
unexpected company.*

Cake

1	pkg (18.25 oz [515 g]) white cake mix	1
1	pkg (4-serving size) vanilla instant pudding mix	1
4	eggs	4
1 1/3 cups	sour cream	325 mL
1/3 cup	vegetable oil	75 mL
1 cup	miniature semi-sweet chocolate chips	250 mL

Topping

1/2 cup	packed brown sugar	125 mL
1/2 cup	grape-nuts-type cereal	125 mL
1/2 tsp	ground cinnamon	2 mL

Chocolate Drizzle (optional)

2	squares (each 1 oz [28 g]) semi-sweet chocolate	21

1. *Cake:* In a large mixer bowl, combine cake mix, pudding mix, eggs, sour cream and oil. Beat on medium speed for 2 minutes or until smooth. Stir in chocolate chips. Spread batter evenly in prepared pan.

2. *Topping:* Combine brown sugar, cereal and cinnamon. Sprinkle evenly over batter. Bake 40 to 50 minutes or until a toothpick inserted in center comes out clean. Cool completely in pan on wire rack.

3. *Drizzle:* Melt chocolate in a saucepan over low heat, or in microwave on Medium for about 1 1/2 minutes. Stir until smooth. Drizzle over cooled cake.

Apricot Glazed Apple Torte

Preheat oven to 350° F (180° C)
11-inch (27 cm) springform pan, greased

Serves 12 to 16

*A not-too-sweet treat that's
very impressive to serve.*

TIP

This cake is best prepared and
enjoyed the same day.

Golden Delicious apples are a
good choice, since they're a
nice size and keep their shape
during baking.

Torte can also be baked in two
8-inch (20 cm) springform pans
for about 45 minutes. Use half of
topping for each cake.

If you only have a 10-inch
(25 cm) pan, use only three-
quarters of the batter or it will
not bake properly.

VARIATION

Replace apricot jam with
strained marmalade.

Cake

1	pkg (18.25 oz [515 g]) white cake mix	1
1	pkg (4-serving size) vanilla instant pudding mix	1
4	eggs	4
1/2 cup	sour cream	125 mL
1/4 cup	vegetable oil	50 mL

Topping

3	large apples, peeled and cored (see Tip, at left)	3
1 tbsp	granulated sugar	15 mL
1 tbsp	ground cinnamon	15 mL
1/3 cup	strained apricot jam	75 mL

1. *Cake:* In a large mixer bowl, combine cake mix, pudding mix, eggs, sour cream and oil. Beat on medium speed for 2 minutes or until smooth. Spread evenly in prepared pan.

2. *Topping:* Slice peeled and cored apples into eighths. Press apple slices round-side up into batter in a circular pattern. Mix sugar and cinnamon. Sprinkle evenly over apples. Bake 60 to 70 minutes or until cake is firm in the center. Remove pan to a wire rack and cool slightly. Warm jam if necessary to soften to a spreading consistency. Brush over top of apples and cake. Serve warm or cool.

Cinnamon Brunch Cake

Preheat oven to 350° F (180° C)
10-inch (3 L) Bundt pan, greased

Serves 12 to 16

This is one of my mother's favorite cakes. I'm not sure if it's because she likes the taste or because I can make it ahead to leave in her freezer!

TIP

If freezing the cake, leave off the drizzle. Serve plain, sprinkle with confectioner's sugar or glaze thawed cake just before serving.

Use a skewer or cake tester to test doneness of tube cakes. Toothpicks are not usually long enough.

VARIATION

Use your favorite kind of nuts. If using pecans or walnuts, replace almond extract with vanilla.

Cake

1/2 cup	packed brown sugar	125 mL
2 tsp	ground cinnamon	10 mL
3/4 cup	finely chopped almonds	175 mL
1	pkg (18.25 oz [515 g]) white cake mix	1
1	pkg (4-serving size) vanilla instant pudding mix	1
4	eggs	4
3/4 cup	vegetable oil	175 mL
3/4 cup	water	175 mL
1 tsp	almond extract	5 mL

Glaze (optional)

1 cup	confectioner's (icing) sugar, sifted	250 mL
1 to 2 tbsp	milk	15 to 25 mL
1/2 tsp	vanilla extract	2 mL

1. *Cake:* Combine brown sugar and cinnamon. Set aside for filling. Sprinkle almonds evenly in bottom of prepared pan. In a large mixer bowl, combine cake mix, pudding mix, eggs, oil, water and almond extract. Beat on medium speed for 2 minutes. Spread one-third of batter over nuts in pan. Sprinkle half of cinnamon-sugar filling over batter. Spread another third of batter on top, remaining filling, then remaining batter. Bake 45 to 55 minutes or until a cake tester inserted in center comes out clean. Cool 25 minutes in pan on a wire rack, then remove cake.

2. *Glaze:* Combine all glaze ingredients, adding enough milk to make a smooth drizzling consistency. Drizzle over cake. Serve warm or cool.

Sour Cream Coffee Cake

Preheat oven to 350° F (180° C)
10-inch (4 L) tube pan, greased and floured

Serves 12 to 16

The sour cream keeps this cake moist making it ideal to prepare for a brunch.

Cake

1	pkg (18.25 oz [515 g]) white cake mix	1
1	pkg (4-serving size) vanilla instant pudding mix	1
4	eggs	4
1 cup	sour cream	250 mL
1/2 cup	vegetable oil	125 mL

Topping

1/3 cup	granulated sugar	75 mL
1 1/2 tsp	ground cinnamon	7 mL
3/4 cup	chopped nuts	175 mL

1. *Cake:* In a large mixer bowl, combine cake mix, pudding mix, eggs, sour cream and oil. Beat on medium speed for 4 minutes.

2. *Topping:* Combine sugar and cinnamon until blended. Stir in nuts.

3. *Assembly:* Spread half of batter in prepared pan. Sprinkle half of topping mixture evenly over batter. Repeat with remaining batter and topping. Bake 50 to 55 minutes or until a cake tester inserted in center comes out clean. Cool 25 minutes in pan on a wire rack, then remove coffee cake from pan. Serve warm or cool.

Apple Sour Cream Coffee Cake

Preheat oven to 350° F (180° C)
13- by 9-inch (3.5 L) cake pan, greased and floured

Serves 12 to 16

A delicious fall cake with fresh tart apples. It's also nice with pears, plums or peaches.

TIP

Slice apples thinly for quick, even baking. You want them to be tender-crisp.

VARIATION

A mixture of other fall fruits gives a different taste and appearance to this versatile batter.

Cake

1	pkg (18.25 oz [515 g]) white cake mix	1
1	egg	1
1 cup	sour cream	250 mL
1/4 cup	butter, melted	50 mL

Topping

3 1/2 cups	thinly sliced apples, (1/4-inch [3 cm] thick) (4 or 5 large apples)	875 mL
1/2 cup	packed brown sugar	125 mL
1 tsp	ground cinnamon	5 mL
1/3 cup	sliced almonds	75 mL
1/4 cup	butter, melted	50 mL

1. *Cake:* In a large mixer bowl, combine cake mix, egg, sour cream and melted butter. Beat on low speed for 1 minute or until a soft dough forms. Spread evenly in prepared pan. Bake 12 minutes.

2. *Topping:* Arrange apple slices over cake base. Combine brown sugar, cinnamon and almonds. Sprinkle evenly over apples. Drizzle melted butter on top. Bake 30 to 35 minutes longer or until golden brown and apples are tender-crisp. Cool at least 30 minutes in pan on a wire rack. Serve warm or cool.

Blueberry Pecan Coffee Cake

Preheat oven to 350° F (180° C)
13- by 9-inch (3.5 L) cake pan, greased

Serves 12 to 16

Enjoy fresh berries at their best – especially with a tender cake underneath and a crunchy nut streusel on top.

TIP

Small wild blueberries are wonderful in this cake. The next best choice is regular fresh berries or, failing these, use frozen berries, thawed and patted dry.

Topping

1/2 cup	packed brown sugar	125 mL
2 tbsp	all-purpose flour	25 mL
1/2 tsp	ground cinnamon	2 mL
1 cup	chopped pecans	250 mL
3 tbsp	butter, melted	45 mL

Cake

1	pkg (18.25 oz [515 g]) white cake mix	1
1/3 cup	granulated sugar	75 mL
8 oz	cream cheese, softened	250 g
3	eggs	3
1/2 cup	vegetable oil	125 mL
1/4 cup	water	50 mL
2 cups	fresh blueberries	500 mL

1. *Topping:* Combine all topping ingredients. Mix well; and set aside.

2. *Cake:* In a large mixer bowl, combine cake mix, sugar, cream cheese, eggs, oil and water. Beat on low speed for 1 minute to blend, then on medium speed for 2 minutes or until smooth. Spread batter evenly in prepared pan. Scatter blueberries evenly over batter. Sprinkle topping over berries. Bake 45 to 50 minutes or until a toothpick inserted in center comes out clean. Cool at least 30 minutes in pan on a wire rack. Serve warm or cool.

Blueberry Coffee Cake

Preheat oven to 375° F (190° C)
13- by 9-inch (3.5 L) cake pan, greased

Serves 12 to 16

*A wonderful way to enjoy
fresh blueberries while they
are in season.*

TIP

If blueberries seem very juicy or
if they've been previously
frozen, toss with a little flour
before putting in cake.

VARIATION

A mixture of blueberries
and raspberries, or all
raspberries, also tastes great.

Streusel		
2/3 cup	all-purpose flour	150 mL
1/2 cup	packed brown sugar	125 mL
1/3 cup	butter, softened	75 mL
1/2 tsp	ground cinnamon	2 mL
Cake		
1	pkg (18.25 oz [515 g]) white cake mix	1
1/3 cup	granulated sugar	75 mL
8 oz	cream cheese, softened	250 g
3	eggs	3
1/2 cup	vegetable oil	125 mL
1/4 cup	water	50 mL
3 cups	fresh blueberries	750 mL

1. *Streusel:* Combine all ingredients for streusel, mixing until crumbly. Set aside.

2. *Cake:* In a large mixer bowl, combine cake mix, sugar, cream cheese, eggs, oil and water. Beat on low speed for 1 minute to blend, then on medium speed for 2 minutes or until smooth. Spread half of batter in prepared pan. Scatter blueberries over batter. Spread remaining batter over berries. Sprinkle streusel evenly over batter. Bake 40 to 45 minutes or until top springs back when lightly touched. Cool at least 30 minutes in pan on a wire rack. Serve warm or cool.

Lemon Streusel Cake

Preheat oven to 375° F (190° C)
10-inch (4 L) tube pan, greased and floured

Serves 12 to 16

The glaze adds a very attractive finish, but it's not necessary if preparation time is tight.

TIP

Another quick drizzle can be made by mixing 3/4 cup (175 mL) ready-to-serve vanilla frosting with 1 tsp (5 mL) lemon juice and 3 drops food coloring. Simply heat in microwave or stove-top just to soften to drizzling consistency.

VARIATION

Replace lemon extract with orange extract for a mixed citrus flavor.

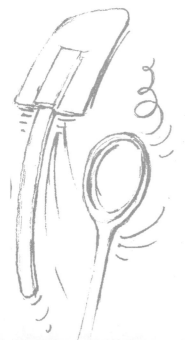

Streusel

1/2 cup	all-purpose flour	125 mL
1/2 cup	confectioner's (icing) sugar, sifted	125 mL
2 tbsp	butter, melted	25 mL
1 tsp	lemon extract	5 mL
3	drops yellow food coloring	3

Cake

1	pkg (18.25 oz [515 g]) lemon cake mix	1
3	eggs	3
1 cup	water	250 mL
1/3 cup	butter, softened	75 mL

Glaze

1 cup	confectioner's (icing) sugar, sifted	250 mL
1 to 2 tbsp	water	15 to 25 mL
1/4 tsp	lemon extract	1 mL
3	drops yellow food coloring	3

1. *Streusel:* Combine all ingredients for streusel. Mix well and set aside.

2. *Cake:* In a large mixer bowl, combine cake mix, eggs, water and butter. Beat on medium speed for 2 minutes. Spread one-third of batter in prepared pan. Sprinkle with one-third of streusel. Repeat layering two more times, ending with streusel. Bake 40 to 50 minutes or until a cake tester inserted in center comes out clean. Cool 25 minutes in pan on a wire rack, then remove cake and cool completely.

3. *Glaze:* Combine all ingredients, adding enough water to make a smooth, drizzling consistency. Drizzle over cake.

Chocolate Banana Coffee Cake

Preheat oven to 350° F (180° C)

13- by 9-inch (3.5 L) cake pan, greased

Serves 12 to 16

Quick, moist and tasty. Perfect for a lunchbox treat.

Cake

1	pkg (18.25 oz [515 g]) white cake mix	1
1	pkg (4-serving size) vanilla instant pudding mix	1
4	eggs	4
1 1/2 cups	mashed ripe bananas (3 or 4 large bananas)	375 mL
1/3 cup	vegetable oil	75 mL

Topping

1/2 cup	packed brown sugar	125 mL
1 tsp	ground cinnamon	5 mL
1 1/2 cups	semi-sweet chocolate chips	375 mL

1. *Cake:* In a large mixer bowl, combine cake mix, pudding mix, eggs, mashed bananas and oil. Beat on medium speed for 2 minutes. Spread half of batter in prepared pan.

2. *Topping:* Combine brown sugar and cinnamon. Sprinkle half over batter in pan. Top with half of the chocolate chips. Repeat layers with remaining cake batter, sugar mixture and chips. Bake 45 to 50 minutes or until a toothpick inserted in center comes out clean. Serve warm or cool.

LOAVES AND MUFFINS

Cranberry Banana Loaf

Preheat oven to 350° F (180° C)
Two 8 1/2- by 4 1/2-inch (1.5 L) loaf pans, greased and floured

Makes about 30 slices

Bananas combine well with other ingredients such as nuts and chocolate chips, but cranberries always seem to be a favorite.

1	pkg (18.25 oz [515 g]) white cake mix	1
4 oz	cream cheese, softened	125 g
1	egg	1
1 1/2 cups	mashed ripe bananas (3 or 4 large bananas)	375 mL
1 1/2 cups	fresh cranberries	375 mL

1. In a large mixer bowl, combine cake mix, cream cheese, egg and mashed bananas. Beat on low speed until smoothly blended, about 2 minutes. Batter will be stiff. Fold in cranberries. Spread batter in prepared pans, dividing evenly. Bake 45 to 50 minutes or until a toothpick inserted in center comes out clean. Cool 20 minutes in pans on a wire rack, then remove loaves and cool completely.

TIP

Use very ripe bananas for the best flavor and texture in baked goods.

VARIATION

Replace cranberries with 3/4 cup (175 mL) chopped nuts or miniature chocolate chips.

Glazed Lemon Loaf

Preheat oven to 350° F (180° C)
Two 8 1/2- by 4 1/2-inch loaf pans, greased and lined with aluminum foil

Makes about 30 slices

*Lemon loaf is an
old-fashioned favorite
for an anytime treat with
coffee or tea.*

Loaf

1	pkg (18.25 oz [515 g]) lemon cake mix	1
3	eggs	3
1 cup + 3 tbsp	water	295 mL
1/3 cup	vegetable oil	75 mL

Glaze

1/2 cup	granulated sugar	125 mL
1/4 cup	lemon juice	50 mL

1. *Loaf:* In a large mixer bowl, combine cake mix, eggs, water and oil. Beat on medium speed for 2 minutes. Spread batter in prepared pans, dividing evenly. Bake 35 to 45 minutes or until a toothpick inserted in center comes out clean. Cool 10 minutes in pans on a wire rack.

2. *Glaze:* Heat sugar and lemon juice together to dissolve sugar. Poke holes in top of loaves with fork or toothpick. Brush glaze on tops, letting it soak in. Cool loaves completely, then remove from pans.

Applesauce Loaf

Preheat oven to 350° F (180° C)
Two 8 1/2- by 4 1/2-inch loaf pans, greased and floured

Makes about 30 slices

A hint of spice is always nice with apples. The addition of dried cranberries or raisins makes it even better in this tender, moist loaf.

VARIATION

Use 1 1/2 tsp (7 mL) pumpkin pie spice in place of cinnamon and nutmeg.

1	pkg (18.25 oz [515 g]) yellow cake mix	1
1	pkg (4-serving size) vanilla instant pudding mix	1
4	eggs	4
1 cup	applesauce	250 mL
1/2 cup	water	125 mL
1/4 cup	vegetable oil	50 mL
1 1/2 tsp	ground cinnamon	7 mL
1/2 tsp	ground nutmeg	2 mL
1 cup	dried cranberries or raisins	250 mL

1. In a large mixer bowl, combine cake mix, pudding mix, eggs, applesauce, water, oil and spices. Beat on low speed for 1 minute to blend, then on medium speed for 3 minutes. Fold in cranberries. Spread batter in prepared pans, dividing evenly. Bake 50 to 60 minutes or until a toothpick inserted in center comes out clean. Cool 20 minutes in pans on a wire rack, then remove loaves and cool completely.

Chocolate Chocolate Chunk Muffins

Preheat oven to 350° F (180° C)
Two 12-cup muffin tins, greased or paper-lined

Makes 24 muffins

1	pkg (18.25 oz [515 g]) deep chocolate cake mix	1
1	pkg (4-serving size) chocolate instant pudding mix	1
4	eggs	4
1 cup	sour cream	250 mL
1/2 cup	water	125 mL
1/3 cup	vegetable oil	75 mL
1 2/3 cups	jumbo chocolate chips	400 mL

Definitely not your "healthy" breakfast muffin – but definitely a favorite treat.

1. In a large mixer bowl, combine cake mix, pudding mix, eggs, sour cream, water and oil. Beat on low speed for 1 minute to blend, then on medium speed for 1 minute. Stir in chocolate chips. Spoon batter into prepared muffin tins. Bake 20 to 25 minutes or until top springs back when lightly touched.

TIP

Paper muffin-cup liners make for easy pan clean-up. They are also excellent to use if you're transporting or freezing the muffins.

VARIATION

Use chocolate chunks, jumbo chips or regular-size chips.

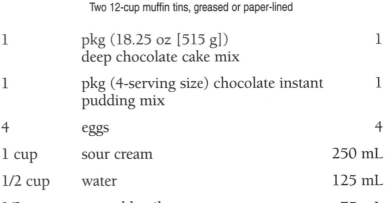

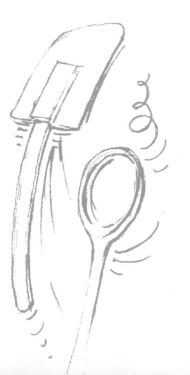

Cranberry Double Banana Muffins

Preheat oven to 375° F (190° C)
Two 12-cup muffin tins, greased or paper lined

Makes 24 muffins

The combination of banana and cranberries is outstanding.

1	pkg (18.25 oz [515 g]) white cake mix	1
1	pkg (4-serving size) banana cream instant pudding mix	1
3	eggs	3
1 1/2 cups	mashed ripe bananas (3 or 4 large bananas)	375 mL
1/4 cup	vegetable oil	50 mL
2 cups	fresh cranberries	500 mL

1. In a large bowl, combine cake mix, pudding mix, eggs, mashed bananas and oil. Stir with a wooden spoon just until blended. Fold in cranberries. Spoon batter into prepared muffins pans. Bake 15 to 20 minutes or until set and golden.

TIP

Muffins containing fresh fruit like cranberries and blueberries are usually quite fragile to remove from pan without paper liners. Cool them completely, then loosen with the tip of a knife, and they'll come out in one piece.

For nicely shaped, uniform-sized muffins, use an ice cream scoop to fill muffin cups.

Don't overmix the batter or the muffins will be tough.

VARIATION

Replace cranberries with blueberries, raisins or nuts.

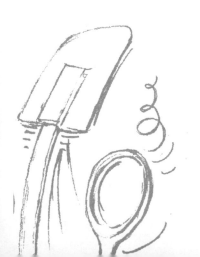

Apple Oatmeal Muffins

Makes 18 muffins

Preheat oven to 375° F (190° C)
One 12-cup and one 6-cup muffin tins, greased or paper lined

1	pkg (18.25 oz [515 g]) white cake mix	1
1 cup	quick-cooking oats	250 mL
2 tsp	ground cinnamon	10 mL
1/2 tsp	baking powder	2 mL
3	eggs	3
1 3/4 cups	chopped peeled, apples (2 large apples)	425 mL
1 1/3 cups	milk	325 mL
1/2 cup	butter, melted	125 mL

A quick and easy way to prepare tender moist muffins for breakfast on the run.

TIP

Keep a bag of baked muffins in the freezer and remove them as you need them. Thaw overnight at room temperature or in the microwave.

If you have only 12-cup muffin tins, fill unused cups 3/4 full of water before baking.

VARIATION

For a different flavor, add raisins or dried cranberries to batter.

1. In a large bowl, combine cake mix, oats, cinnamon and baking powder. Stir to blend. In another large bowl, whisk together eggs, apples, milk and melted butter. Add dry ingredients, stirring with a wooden spoon just until blended. Spoon batter into prepared muffins tins. Bake 20 to 25 minutes or until set and golden.

Blueberry Muffins

Preheat oven to 375° F (190° C)
Two 12-cup muffin tins, greased or paper lined

Makes 18 muffins

When available, wild blueberries are wonderful in muffins.

1	pkg (18.25 oz [515 g]) lemon cake mix	1
1/4 cup	all-purpose flour	50 mL
1 tsp	baking powder	5 mL
3	eggs	3
2/3 cup	milk	150 mL
1/3 cup	vegetable oil	75 mL
1 1/2 cups	fresh blueberries	375 mL

1. In a bowl combine cake mix, flour and baking powder. Stir to blend. In a large bowl, whisk eggs, milk and oil. Add dry ingredients, stirring just until blended. Fold in blueberries. Spoon batter into prepared muffin pans. Bake 17 to 23 minutes or until set and golden.

TIP

Frozen blueberries, thawed and patted dry, can be used if fresh are not available. If blueberries are wet, toss with a spoonful of flour before mixing into batter.

Keep a bag of baked muffins in the freezer and remove them as you need them. Thaw overnight at room temperature or in the microwave.

VARIATION

Replace blueberries with cranberries.

If lemon isn't a favorite, try a white cake mix for another great taste.

APRICOT GLAZED APPLE TORTE (PAGE 81) ➤
OVERLEAF: ORANGE SOUFFLÉ CAKE (PAGE 114)

SPECIAL OCCASION CAKES

◄ SOUR CREAM COFFEE CAKE (PAGE 83)

Apricot Almond Angel Roll

Preheat oven to 350° F (180° C)
15- by 10-inch (2 L) jelly roll pan, greased, lined with parchment or
waxed paper and greased again
8-inch (2 L) square cake pan,
ungreased and lined with parchment or waxed paper

Serves 8 to 12

It's hard to believe this light, creamy dessert roll starts with an angel food cake mix.

Cake
1	pkg (16 oz [450 g]) white angel food cake mix	1

Filling
1 1/2 cups	whipping (35%) cream	375 mL
2 tbsp	confectioner's (icing) sugar, sifted	25 mL
1/2 tsp	almond extract	2 mL
1	can (14 oz [398 mL]) apricot halves, drained and coarsely chopped (1 cup [250 mL])	1
1/2 cup	toasted slivered almonds	125 mL

1. *Cake:* Prepare cake mix according to package directions. Remove 3 cups (750 mL) batter and spread it in prepared square pan. Spread remaining batter evenly in jelly roll pan. Bake cakes about 20 minutes or until set, golden and top springs back when lightly touched. Cool 10 minutes in pan on a wire rack, then invert cakes onto tea towels sprinkled with confectioner's sugar. Remove pans and paper. Store square cake for another use. Starting from short side, loosely roll up jelly roll in the tea towel. Cool completely.

2. *Filling:* In a small mixer bowl, beat cream, confectioner's sugar and extract together until stiff peaks form. Remove half and set aside for topping. Fold apricot pieces into remaining cream.

3. *Assembly:* Unroll cake carefully. Spread with apricot cream mixture. Re-roll and place on a serving dish, seam-side down. Frost cake completely with reserved cream. Sprinkle toasted almonds on top. Chill until serving. Store leftover cake in refrigerator.

Pumpkin Pie Crunch

Preheat oven to 350° F (180° C)
13- by 9-inch (3.5 L) cake pan, greased

Serves 12 to 16

It doesn't have to be Thanksgiving to enjoy this dessert.

TIP

For 1 tbsp (15 mL) pumpkin pie spice, you can use a combination of 2 tsp (10 mL) ground cinnamon and 1/2 tsp (2 mL) each ground nutmeg and ground cloves.

VARIATION

Replace pecans with walnuts, hazelnuts or almonds.

1	can (14 oz [398 mL]) pumpkin purée (not pie filling)	1
2	eggs	2
1 1/2 cups	evaporated milk	375 mL
1 1/3 cups	granulated sugar	325 mL
1 tbsp	pumpkin pie spice	15 mL
1/2 tsp	salt	2 mL
1	pkg (18.25 oz [515 g]) yellow cake mix	1
1 1/4 cups	coarsely chopped pecans	300 mL
1 cup	butter, melted	250 mL
	Whipped cream	

1. In a large mixing bowl, stir together pumpkin, eggs, evaporated milk, sugar, spice and salt until smoothly blended. Pour into prepared pan. Sprinkle dry cake mix evenly on top. Scatter nuts over cake mix. Drizzle melted butter over nuts, moistening dry mixture as much as possible. Bake 50 to 60 minutes or until set and golden. Cool at least 1 hour in pan on a wire rack before serving. Serve with whipped cream. Store left-over dessert in refrigerator.

Chocolate Fruit Cake

Preheat oven to 275° F (140° C)
Two 9- by 5-inch (2 L) loaf pans, greased and lined with greased brown paper
or aluminum foil

Makes about 60 slices

Different and delicious. It makes a great combination on a tray with a light cake such as LIGHT BRAZIL NUT FRUITCAKE (see recipe, facing page).

1 1/2 cups	chopped dates	375 mL
1 1/2 cups	chopped candied cherries	375 mL
1 cup	chopped candied pineapple	250 mL
1 cup	raisins	250 mL
1 cup	coarsely chopped pecans	250 mL
1 cup	all-purpose flour	250 mL
1	pkg (18.25 oz [515 g]) devil's food cake mix	1
3	eggs	3
2/3 cup	water	150 mL
1/2 cup	sherry	125 mL
1/2 cup	vegetable oil	125 mL

TIP

Store fruit cake at least one week before slicing. It will become moist and mellow, and improve in flavor. If desired, poke holes with a skewer in cooled cake and brush with warm brandy. Wrap in cheesecloth and store tightly covered in a cool, dry place.

It's easiest to cut fruit cakes when they are cold.

This is a rich cake so you may want to cut each slice into halves or thirds.

VARIATION

Replace walnuts and pecans with almonds.

Replace sherry with brandy or rum.

1. In a large bowl, combine fruit, nuts and flour. Mix well. Set aside. In a large mixer bowl, combine cake mix, eggs, water, sherry and oil. Beat on medium speed for 2 minutes. Pour batter over fruit mixture. Mix well. Spread batter evenly in prepared pans. Bake 2 1/4 hours or until a toothpick inserted in center comes out clean. Cool 30 minutes in pans on a wire rack, then remove cakes from pans, remove paper and cool completely. Wrap airtight in plastic and store in refrigerator.

Light Brazil Nut Fruitcake

Preheat oven to 300° F (150° C)
Two 9- by 5-inch (2 L) loaf pans, greased and lined with greased brown paper
or aluminum foil

Makes about 60 slices

*A very attractive cake that's
crammed full of large
chunks of brazil nuts and
fruit, held together with
a little batter.*

2 cups	candied cherries, halved	500 mL
1 1/2 cups	light raisins	375 mL
1 1/2 cups	diced candied pineapple	375 mL
1 1/2 cups	coarsely chopped Brazil nuts	375 mL
1 cup	mixed candied fruit	250 mL
1/4 cup	all-purpose flour	50 mL
1	pkg (18.25 oz [515 g]) white cake mix	1
1	pkg (4-serving size) vanilla instant pudding mix	1
3	eggs	3
1/2 cup	water	125 mL
1/3 cup	vegetable oil	75 mL
1 tsp	lemon extract	5 mL

1. *Cake:* In a large bowl, combine fruit, nuts and flour.
   Mix well. Set aside. In a large mixer bowl, combine
   cake mix, pudding mix, eggs, water, oil and lemon
   extract Beat on medium speed for 2 minutes. Pour
   batter over fruit mixture. Mix well. Spread batter
   evenly in prepared pans. Bake 1 1/2 hours or until
   toothpick inserted in center comes out clean. Cool for
   30 minutes in pans on wire rack then remove from
   pans, remove paper and cool completely. Wrap airtight
   in plastic and store in refrigerator. Cut in slices, then
   cut each slice in half or thirds.

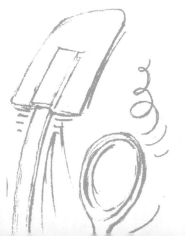

Medium Holiday Fruitcake

Preheat oven to 300° F (150° C)
Two 9- by 5-inch (2 L) loaf pans, greased and lined with greased brown paper or
aluminum foil

Makes about 60 slices

*If you make only one kind
of fruitcake, this medium
colored cake is a good
choice.*

TIP

When testing fruitcake for
doneness, the toothpick or
skewer may be sticky from the
fruit but it shouldn't be gooey
with batter. Remember the cake
will continue to cook a little after
you take it out of the oven.
If top is becoming too brown,
cover it with foil for last part of
the baking.

Brush cooled cake with
warm corn syrup and decorate
with candied fruit and nuts,
if desired.

Cut slices of this rich cake into
halves or thirds for serving.

VARIATION

Deluxe types of mixed fruit
usually contain cherries and
pineapple, so you may want to
eliminate these ingredients and
use 4 1/2 cups (1.13 L) of the
deluxe mix.

2 1/2 cups	cut mixed candied fruit	625 mL
1 1/2 cups	raisins	375 mL
1 1/4 cups	chopped candied cherries	300 mL
3/4 cup	chopped candied pineapple	175 mL
1 1/2 cups	coarsely chopped nuts	375 mL
1/2 cup	all-purpose flour	125 mL
1	pkg (18.25 oz [515 g]) spice cake mix	1
1	pkg (4-serving size) vanilla instant pudding mix	1
3	eggs	3
1/2 cup	vegetable oil	125 mL
1/4 cup	water	50 mL

1. In a large bowl, combine fruit, nuts and flour. Mix
well. Set aside. In a large mixer bowl, combine cake mix,
pudding mix, eggs, oil and water. Beat on medium speed
for 2 minutes. Pour batter over fruit mixture. Mix well.
Spread batter evenly in prepared pans. Bake 1 1/2 hours
or until a toothpick inserted in center comes out clean.
(See Tip, at left.). Cool 30 minutes in pans on a wire
rack, then remove from pans, remove paper and cool
completely. Wrap airtight in plastic and store in
refrigerator.

Choo Choo Train Birthday Cake

Preheat oven to 350° F (180° C)
Six 4 1/2- by 2 3/4-inches (250 mL) mini loaf pans, greased and floured
One 8-inch (2 L) square *or* 9-inch (1.5 L) round cake pan

Serves 12 to 18

Let kids help decorate their own party cake. They love it for birthdays, but it is also a fun rainy-day project. Use (see page 64, overleaf) picture to give them ideas to start. Leave the rest to their imagination.

(see page 64, overleaf)

1	pkg (18.25 oz [515 g]) cake mix, any flavor	1
2	containers (each 15 oz [450 g]) ready-to-serve chocolate frosting	2

Assorted candies to decorate (eg. round mints, cinnamon hearts, marshmallows, Smarties, Lifesavers, gum drops, nuts, colored sprinkles, etc.)

String licorice (black) for train track

1. *Cake:* Prepare cake mix as directed on package. Fill each loaf pan half full of batter. Pour remaining batter into square or round cake pan. Bake loaves 18 to 23 minutes and large cake as directed on package. Cool 15 minutes on a wire rack, then remove from pans and cool completely. Freeze large cake for future use.

2. *Assembly:* Place loaf cakes upside down on a foil-lined board, a baking sheet or on cardboard. Frost top and sides of loaves with chocolate frosting. Decorate train engine with candle smokestack. Put round candy wheels on each car. Fill top of remaining 5 cars with small candies or sprinkles. Place licorice on board between cars for the railway track.

TIP

If foil mini loaf pans aren't available, bake cake in square or rectangular pans as directed on package, then cut into 6 small rectangles.

Use birthday candles for the smoke stack.

Cut one of the cakes in half for a caboose.

Make up the number of mini cakes to match the size of your party.

VARIATION

Vary the train colors with different colored frostings.

Cupcakes Galore

Preheat oven to 350° F (180° C)
Line 24 muffin cups with large paper liners

Makes 24 cupcakes

1	pkg (18.25 oz [515 g]) cake mix, any flavor	1
1 or 2	containers (each 15 oz [450 g]) ready-to-serve vanilla frosting	1 or 2
1 or 2	containers (each 15 oz [450 g]) ready-to-serve chocolate frosting	1 or 2

A great way to entertain kids at a birthday party. Let them decorate their own dessert.

TIP

Set up bowls containing a variety of icings and colorful candies for decorating. Have a few made up to get the ideas flowing, then leave the rest to the creator's imagination.

VARIATION

Vary the kind of cake and icing to suit the items being made.

1. Prepare, bake and cool cupcakes as directed on package. Frost and decorate as desired using the ideas below to get you started.

Butterfly Cupcakes: With a paring knife, remove cone-shaped piece from top center of each cupcake. Fill hollow with lemon curd, whipped cream or whipped dessert topping. Cut reserved cake cone in half. Press into filling for butterfly wings. Dust with confectioner's icing sugar.

Animal Faces: Frost top of cupcake with vanilla or chocolate frosting. Create funny faces using round candies, licorice, nuts, ju jubes, sprinkles, etc.

Half-and-Half Cupcakes: Prepare cupcakes using a white cake mix and a chocolate cake mix. Remove paper liners. Cut white and chocolate cupcakes in half vertically. Spread cut surfaces with frosting. Press a white and a chocolate half together and frost tops. Decorate as desired.

Christmas Picture Cupcakes: Cut a small cardboard pattern of a star, tree, etc. Then either (a) for each light-colored cupcake, place pattern on cupcake and sift sweetened cocoa mix over top. Carefully lift off pattern. For dark colored cupcakes, sift confectioner's (icing) sugar on the pattern. Or, (b) frost cupcake and place pattern on top. Sprinkle red or green colored sugar or cake sprinkles on top, pressing lightly into frosting. Lift off pattern.

Snowball Cupcakes: Spread top and sides of cupcakes with white frosting. Sprinkle or roll in flaked coconut.

Alphabet or Number Cupcakes: Spread top of cupcakes with white frosting. Use string licorice cut into short pieces to make numbers or letters on top. It's a fun way to help children learn numbers and their ABCs.

Pumpkin Cake

Preheat oven to 350° F (180° C)

13- by 9-inch (3.5 L) cake pan, greased and floured

Serves 12 to 16

A moist spice cake with a mild pumpkin taste. It will be a favorite for those who don't like pumpkin pie.

1	pkg (18.25 oz [515 g]) spice cake mix	1
1	pkg (4-serving size) vanilla instant pudding mix	1
4	eggs	4
1 1/3 cups	pumpkin purée (not pie filling)	325 mL
1/3 cup	vegetable oil	75 mL
1/4 cup	water	50 mL
3/4 tsp	ground cinnamon	4 mL

1. In a large mixer bowl, combine cake mix, pudding mix, eggs, pumpkin, oil, water and cinnamon. Beat on medium speed for 2 minutes. Spread batter evenly in prepared pan. Bake 35 to 40 minutes or until a toothpick inserted in center comes out clean. Cool completely in pan on a wire rack.

TIP

A cream cheese frosting is a good choice but a close second is a plain butter frosting with a hint of cinnamon. Candy pumpkins make a cute decoration.

VARIATION

Bake cake in 2 round layers for about 35 minutes.

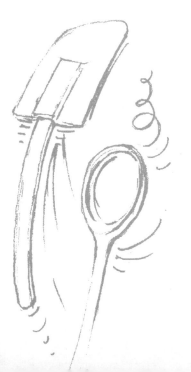

Chocolate Yule Log

Preheat oven to 350° F (180° C)
17 1/2- by 11 1/2- by 1-inch (3 L) jelly roll pan, greased and lined with
parchment paper, leaving an overhang at the sides; grease bottom of parchment.

Serves 12 to 16

A normally intimidating recipe is really quite easy when you start with a cake mix. It's large and decadent – a perfect choice for the holiday season.

TIP

Cover a large board or stiff cardboard with foil for a serving plate. Decorate the board with plastic evergreens and holly.

This makes a very large dessert. You may prefer to fill it and divide it in half. Frost each half separately. Use one and freeze the other for later.

VARIATION

Flavor the filling with rum, brandy or coffee liqueur, if desired.

Replace cream filling with VERY CREAMY BUTTER FROSTING (see recipe, page 162).

Cake

1	pkg (18.25 oz [515 g]) dark chocolate cake mix	1
4	eggs	4
1 cup	plain yogurt	250 mL
1/2 cup	vegetable oil	125 mL
	Confectioner's (icing) sugar	

Filling

2 cups	whipping (35%) cream	500 mL
1/4 cup	confectioner's (icing) sugar, sifted	50 mL
1 tsp	vanilla extract	5 mL

Frosting

1	container (15 oz [450 g]) ready-to-serve chocolate frosting	1

1. *Cake:* In a large mixer bowl, combine cake mix, eggs, yogurt and oil. Beat on medium speed for 2 minutes. Spread batter evenly in prepared pan. Bake 15 to 20 minutes or until cake springs back when lightly touched. Dust a large tea towel with confectioner's sugar. Invert cake pan onto tea towel. Remove pan and carefully peel off paper. While cake is hot, starting from long side and using towel to help, roll up cake loosely in towel. Let cool at least 30 minutes.

2. *Filling:* Beat whipping cream, confectioner's sugar and vanilla to stiff peaks.

3. *Assembly:* Carefully unroll cake and towel. Spread filling evenly over cake. Re-roll cake. (Don't worry about any cracks; they'll be covered with frosting.) Place seam-side down on serving board. Cut a thin slice from each end to make them even. Use centers of these slices for log bumps. Attach to log with a bit of frosting. Cover log, including ends and bumps, with frosting. Run tines of a fork along icing, making lines to resemble bark. Chill until serving. Store leftover log in refrigerator.

Pumpkin Cupcakes

Preheat oven to 350° F (180° C)
Line 24 muffin cups with large paper liners

Makes 24 cupcakes

An ideal treat for Halloween and Thanksgiving parties.

Cupcake

1	pkg (18.25 oz [515 g]) spice cake mix	1
3	eggs	3
1 3/4 cups	pumpkin purée (not pie filling)	425 mL
1/2 cup	water	125 mL
1/3 cup	vegetable oil	75 mL

Decoration

1	container (15 oz [450 g]) vanilla ready-to-serve frosting	1
	Orange food coloring (optional)	
	Colorful candies	

1. *Cupcakes:* In a large mixer bowl, combine cake mix, eggs, pumpkin, water and oil. Beat on medium speed for 2 minutes. Spoon batter into prepared muffin cups, filling three-quarters full. Bake 15 to 20 minutes or until tops spring back when lightly touched. Cool 15 minutes in pans on a wire rack, then remove cupcakes and cool completely.

2. *Decoration:* Color frosting orange if desired. Spread frosting on top of cupcakes. Decorate with your choice of colorful candies.

DESSERTS

Raspberry Angel Dome

Preheat oven to 325° F (160° C)
10-inch (4 L) tube pan, ungreased
Large bowl lined with plastic wrap

Serves 12 to 16

This spectacular dessert is prepared a day ahead, making it ideal for entertaining.

TIP

Be sure to use a clean, ungreased pan or the cake will not rise properly.

Fresh fruit is nice but not essential to the recipe. You can use canned fruit with other flavored juices or leave out the fruit altogether.

VARIATION

Replace raspberry juice concentrate with other frozen juice concentrates such as cranberry, pineapple-orange or fruit punch. Cans vary in size, so keep the amount to about 1 1/2 cups (350 mL).

Cake

1	pkg (16 oz [450 g]) white angel food cake mix	1

Filling & Topping

2	envelopes (each 7 g [1 tbsp/15 mL]) unflavored gelatin	2
1/2 cup	granulated sugar	125 mL
1	can (12 oz [341 mL]) frozen raspberry juice concentrate, thawed	1
2 cups	water	500 mL
2 cups	whipping (35%) cream	500 mL
1 cup	fresh raspberries (optional)	250 mL
3/4 cup	toasted flaked coconut (optional)	175 mL

1. *Cake:* Prepare, bake and cool angel food cake according to package directions. With an electric knife or a long, sharp, serrated knife, cut cake into 1-inch (2.5 cm) cubes. Set aside.

2. *Filling & Topping:* In a small saucepan, combine gelatin and sugar. Stir in juice and water. Bring to a boil, stirring constantly until dissolved. Chill until mixture is starting to set. In a large mixer bowl on high speed, beat 1 cup (250 mL) cream to stiff peaks. Beat gelatin mixture until light and fluffy, about 5 minutes. Fold in whipped cream and raspberries. Put one-third of cake cubes in large bowl lined with plastic wrap. Cover with one-third of gelatin mixture, pressing down lightly to moisten cake cubes. Repeat layering. Cover with plastic wrap. Chill overnight.

3. *Assembly:* Turn out dessert rounded side up onto a serving plate. Remove plastic wrap. Beat remaining 1 cup (250 mL) cream to stiff peaks. Spread evenly over dessert dome. Sprinkle with coconut, if desired. Chill until serving. Store leftover dessert in refrigerator.

Triple Orange Delight

Preheat oven to 325° F (160° C)
10-inch (4 L) tube pan, ungreased
13- by 9-inch (3.5 L) cake pan, lined with plastic wrap

Serves 12 to 16

*A perfect make-ahead
dessert for pot luck dinners.*

Cake

1	pkg (16 oz [450 g]) white angel food cake mix	1

Filling

2	cans (each 10 oz [284 mL]) mandarin orange segments, drained, juice reserved	2
1 cup	reserved mandarin orange juice	250 mL
2	pkgs (each 3 oz [85 g]) orange-flavored gelatin dessert mix	2
4 cups	orange sherbet, softened	1 L
4 cups	frozen whipped topping, thawed	1 L

1. *Cake:* Prepare, bake and cool angel food cake according to package directions. With an electric knife or a long, sharp, serrated knife, cut cake into 1-inch (2.5 cm) cubes. Set aside.

2. *Filling:* Set drained mandarins aside. Bring reserved juice to a boil. Add gelatin, stirring until dissolved. Pour into a large bowl. Add sherbet, stirring until melted. Fold in 2 cups (500 mL) whipped topping gently but thoroughly.

3. *Assembly:* Place half of cake cubes in rectangular pan lined with plastic wrap. Use enough cubes to cover bottom of pan completely. Reserve 12 to 16 mandarins for garnish. Coarsely chop remaining mandarins. Scatter half the mandarins over cake in pan. Cover with half the sherbet mixture. Repeat with remaining cake, mandarins and sherbet mixture. Press down lightly to moisten all cake pieces with sherbet mixture. Cover with plastic wrap and chill overnight. Invert dessert onto a serving plate. Decorate with remaining whipped topping and reserved mandarins. Chill until serving. Store leftover dessert in refrigerator.

Strawberry Bavarian Mold

Preheat oven to 325° F (160° C)
10-inch (4 L) tube pan, ungreased

Serves 12 to 16

Bright red berries with whipped cream on puffs of angel food cake combine to make a show-stopping dessert.

Cake

1	pkg (16 oz [450 g]) white angel food cake mix	1

Filling

16 oz	frozen strawberries, thawed, drained and juice reserved	454 g
1 1/4 cups	strawberry juice (from above), plus water as necessary	300 mL
1	envelope (7 g [1 tbsp/15 mL]) unflavored gelatin	1
1/2 cup	granulated sugar	125 mL
1 tbsp	lemon juice	15 mL
2 cups	whipping (35%) cream	500 mL
2 tbsp	confectioner's (icing) sugar, sifted	25 mL

1. *Cake:* Prepare, bake and cool angel food cake according to package directions. Wash pan and grease for dessert assembly. With an electric knife or a long, sharp, serrated knife, cut cake into 1-inch (2.5 cm) cubes. Set aside.

2. *Filling:* Chop berries coarsely; set aside. In a small saucepan, combine gelatin, sugar, strawberry juice and lemon juice. Bring to a boil, stirring to dissolve gelatin. Chill to consistency of unbeaten egg whites. In a large mixer bowl, beat gelatin mixture on high speed until fluffy, about 5 minutes. Beat 1 cup (250 mL) whipping cream to stiff peaks. Fold whipped cream and reserved strawberries into gelatin mixture.

3. *Assembly:* Place one-third of cake cubes in greased tube pan. Cover with one-third strawberry mixture, pressing down lightly to moisten cake. Repeat layering until all ingredients are used. Cover with plastic wrap; chill overnight. To serve, dip pan quickly in warm water to loosen gelatin. Unmold upside down onto a serving plate. Whip remaining cream and confectioner's sugar to stiff peaks. Frost cake completely. Garnish if desired. Chill until serving. Store leftover dessert in refrigerator.

Chocolate Refrigerator Dessert

Preheat oven to 350° F (180° C)
10-inch (4 L) tube pan or 13- by 9-inch (3.5 L) cake pan, greased and floured
10-inch (25 cm) springform pan, greased

Serves 12 to 16

Lots of chocolate keeps everyone content. This creamy, chocolate dessert doesn't resemble cake at all. It's a nice change for a special occasion.

1	pkg (18.25 oz [515 g]) devil's food cake mix	1
1 1/2 cups	semi-sweet chocolate chips, melted and cooled	375 mL
3	eggs, separated	3
2 tbsp	granulated sugar	25 mL
4 cups	prepared whipped topping	1 L
	Whipped topping or cream to decorate	

1. *Cake:* Prepare and bake cake in tube pan or rectangular pan according to package directions. Cool and remove from pan as directed. With a long, sharp knife cut cake into 1-inch (2.5 cm) pieces. Set aside.

2. *Assembly:* Combine melted chocolate chips, egg yolks and sugar (mixture will be stiff). Beat egg whites to stiff (but not dry) peaks. Stir one-quarter of egg whites into chocolate mixture thoroughly to soften, then fold remaining egg whites and whipped topping into chocolate mixture. Layer cake pieces and chocolate cream mixture in springform pan, pressing down lightly to cover cake with cream. Cover and chill 24 hours. Unmold onto a serving plate and decorate with additional whipped topping or cream as desired.

TIP

This dessert must be made at least a day in advance.

Prepare an extra cake when you have some spare time. With a few standard ingredients on hand you can put this dessert together easily.

Springform pans come in many sizes. If yours is smaller than 10 inches (25 cm), wrap a foil collar around it to extend the height.

You can bake the cake in any size pan recommended on the package.

VARIATION

Use any flavor of chocolate cake. Swiss chocolate is good.

Replace whipped topping with 2 cups (500 mL) whipping (35%) cream, beaten to stiff peaks.

Orange Soufflé Cake

Preheat oven to 350° F (180° C)
Two 9-inch (1.5 L) round cake pans, greased and floured
10-inch (25 cm) or 9 1/2-inch (24 cm) springform pan

Serves 12 to 16

Light and refreshing, this cake is ideal for summer entertaining or to finish a heavy meal.

Cake

1	pkg (18.25 oz [515 g]) white cake mix	1
2	eggs	2
1	can (10 oz [284 mL]) mandarin oranges, drained, juice reserved	1
1/2 cup	mandarin orange juice (from above)	125 mL

Mousse Filling

2	envelopes (each 7 g [1 tbsp/15 mL]) unflavored gelatin	2
1/2 cup	cold water	125 mL
6	eggs	6
3/4 cup	granulated sugar	175 mL
2/3 cup	orange juice	150 mL
2 tbsp	lemon juice	25 mL
1 tbsp	grated orange zest	15 mL
1 cup	whipping (35%) cream	250 mL
	Whipped cream rosettes (optional)	
	Mandarin orange segments (optional)	

1. *Cake:* In a large mixer bowl, combine cake mix, eggs, drained mandarins and juice. Beat on medium speed for 2 minutes or until smooth. Spread in 2 prepared round cake pans, dividing evenly. Bake 25 to 30 minutes or until a toothpick inserted in center comes out clean. Cool 10 minutes in pans on a wire rack then remove layers and cool completely. Freeze 1 cake layer for later use. With a long, sharp knife, cut remaining cake horizontally in half.

2. *Filling:* In a small bowl, sprinkle gelatin over cold water. Let stand 10 minutes to soften. Heat just to dissolve. Cool slightly. In a large mixer bowl, beat eggs and sugar together on high speed until very thick, about 7 minutes. Stir in orange juice, lemon juice, zest and gelatin. Mix well. Chill 10 minutes. Beat cream to soft peaks. Fold into gelatin mixture.

3. *Assembly:* Center bottom cake layer in springform pan (there will be a little room around the edge). Pour half of mousse filling over cake, letting it fill around the sides. Chill 10 minutes. Place remaining cake layer on top, and pour rest of mousse over. Chill until set, 4 hours or overnight.

4. *To Serve:* Run knife around inside rim of pan. Remove pan ring. If desired, decorate top with rosettes of whipped cream and place a mandarin on each rosette. Chill until serving. Store leftover cake in refrigerator.

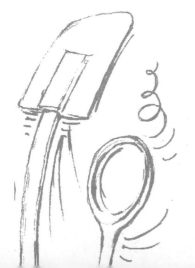

Chocolate Caramel Cream Dessert

Preheat oven to 350° F (180° C)
13- by 9-inch (3.5 L) cake pan, greased

Serves 12 to 16

Definite indulgence. Don't even think about the calories – you can diet tomorrow (and the next day!).

1	pkg (18.25 oz [515 g]) devil's food cake mix	1
1	can (14 oz [398 mL]) sweetened condensed milk	1
1 1/2 cups	toffee bits	375 mL
1 1/4 cups	caramel sundae sauce	300 mL
2 cups	whipping (35%) cream	500 mL
1 cup	milk chocolate chips	250 mL

1. Prepare and bake cake in prepared cake pan according to package directions. Cool completely in pan on a wire rack. Poke holes with end of wooden spoon, about 1 inch (2.5 cm) deep and 1 inch (2.5 cm) apart over entire surface of cake. Pour sweetened condensed milk on top. Sprinkle half the toffee bits on top. Pour caramel sauce on top. Beat whipping cream to stiff peaks. Spread evenly over cake. Sprinkle chocolate chips and remaining toffee bits over cream. Chill until serving. Store leftover dessert in refrigerator.

TIP

Buy a good caramel sauce that is quite thick. The runny ones will make the dessert too soggy. If your sauce seems thin, reduce the amount used to 1 cup (250 mL).

Prepare the cake ahead and freeze. Thaw and finish whenever the occasion arises.

Toffee bits (such as Skor Bits or Heath Bits) can be found where chocolate chips are sold.

VARIATION

Replace milk chocolate chips and toffee bits on top of the cake with crushed crisp toffee chocolate bars such as Skor or Heath.

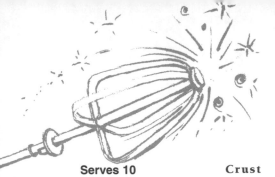

Peach Cobbler

Preheat oven to 350° F (180° C)
13- by 9-inch (3.5 L) cake pan, greased

Serves 10

Canned peach slices also work in this recipe, although the flavor can't compare to fresh.

TIP

If spice cake mix is hard to find – or too spicy for your taste – you can use a white cake mix and add 2 tsp (10 mL) ground cinnamon and 1 tsp (5 mL) ground nutmeg.

VARIATION

Other fruits also work well in cobblers. Try apples, plums and nectarines.

Add 1 cup (250 mL) cranberries to peaches.

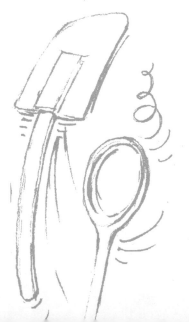

Crust

1	pkg (18.25 oz [515 g]) spice cake mix	1
1 cup	quick-cooking oats	250 mL
1 cup	chopped walnuts	250 mL
3/4 cup	butter, melted	175 mL

Filling

6 cups	sliced peeled peaches (7 large peaches)	1.5 L
1/2 cup	water	125 mL
1/4 cup	packed brown sugar	50 mL
2 tbsp	cornstarch	25 mL
4 tsp	lemon juice	20 mL

1. *Crust:* Combine dry cake mix, oats, walnuts and melted butter. Mix well. Press 2 1/2 cups (625 mL) of crumble mixture firmly into bottom of prepared pan. Set aside remaining crumbs for topping.

2. *Filling:* In a saucepan combine peaches, water and brown sugar. Simmer over low heat for 5 minutes, stirring occasionally. Mix cornstarch and lemon juice until smooth. Add to peaches. Cook, stirring, until thickened. Pour over crust. Sprinkle reserved crumbs over fruit. Bake 25 to 30 minutes or until topping is lightly browned. Serve warm.

Apple Cherry Almond Dessert

Preheat oven to 350° F (180° C)
13- by 9-inch (3.5 L) cake pan, greased

Serves 12 to 16

With this recipe and a few convenience products on hand, dessert is never a problem.

1	can (19 oz [540 mL]) cherry pie filling	1
1	can (19 oz [540 mL]) apple pie filling	1
1	pkg (18.25 oz [515 g]) white cake mix	1
1 cup	quick-cooking oats	250 mL
1/2 cup	packed brown sugar	125 mL
1 cup	coarsely chopped almonds	250 mL
3/4 cup	butter, melted	175 mL

1. In prepared pan, mix cherry and apple pie fillings. Combine dry cake mix, oats, brown sugar and almonds. Sprinkle evenly over fruit. Pour melted butter evenly over crumble mixture, moistening crumbs as much as possible. Bake 50 to 60 minutes or until golden. Serve warm.

TIP

Fruit desserts like crisps and cobblers should be served the same day they are baked. In fact, they are best when eaten warm from the oven.

Prepare the crumble mixture ahead for easy assembly.

VARIATION

Try this recipe using all cherry or all apple filling. Or use 2 cans of any fruit pie filling that suits your family's taste.

Cheery Cherry Cobbler

Preheat oven to 350° F (180° C)
13- by 9-inch (3.5 L) cake pan, greased

Serves 12 to 16

*In this fascinating dessert,
the cake and fruit layers
reverse during baking.*

TIP

Cornstarch and flour can both
be used for thickening. To
replace cornstarch, you'll need
about twice as much flour.

A few drops of red food coloring
in the fruit mixture gives it a
brighter color.

VARIATION

Omit almond extract if desired.

Crust

1	pkg (18.25 oz [515 g]) white cake mix	1
3	eggs	3
1 1/4 cups	water	300 mL
1/3 cup	vegetable oil	75 mL

Fruit Filling

1 cup	granulated sugar	250 mL
2 tbsp	cornstarch	25 mL
1	jar (28 oz [796 mL]) pitted red tart cherries, with juice	1
2 tbsp	butter, melted	25 mL
1/2 tsp	almond extract (optional)	2 mL
	Whipped cream *or* ice cream (optional)	

1. *Crust:* In a large mixer bowl, combine cake mix, eggs, water and oil. Beat on medium speed for 2 minutes. Spread evenly in prepared pan.

2. *Fruit Filling:* In a medium bowl, combine sugar and cornstarch. Stir in cherries (with juice), melted butter and extract. Mix well. Spoon evenly over batter. Bake 50 to 60 minutes or until cake is set and golden. Serve warm or cool with whipped cream or ice cream, if desired.

Lemon Pineapple Cake Dessert

Preheat oven to 350° F (180° C)
13- by 9-inch (3.5 L) cake pan

Serves 12 to 16

This dessert may not take a prize for appearance, but with its great taste and ease of preparation, who cares?

1	can (14 oz [398 mL]) crushed pineapple, with juice	1
1	pkg (18.25 oz [515 g]) lemon cake mix	1
1	egg	1
1/4 cup	granulated sugar	50 mL
1 1/3 cups	water	325 mL
1/3 cup	vegetable oil	75 mL
1 tsp	vanilla extract	5 mL

1. Spread pineapple and juice evenly in pan. Sprinkle dry cake mix on top. In a small mixer bowl, combine egg, sugar, water, oil and vanilla. Beat on medium speed for 1 minute or until smoothly blended. Pour evenly over cake mix; do not stir. Bake 30 to 35 minutes or until golden brown. Serve warm or cool.

Black Forest Trifle

Preheat oven to 350° F (180° C)
13- by 9-inch (3.5 L) cake pan, greased
Trifle bowl or large glass serving bowl

Serves 12 to 16

The favorite Black Forest Cake with a new look!

1	pkg (18.25 oz [515 g]) chocolate cake mix	1
1	pkg (6-serving size) chocolate pudding and pie filling (not instant)	1
4 cups	milk	1 L
1	can (19 oz [540 mL]) cherry pie filling	1
6 tbsp	cherry liqueur	90 mL
2 cups	whipping (35%) cream	500 mL
	Maraschino cherries	
	Shaved chocolate	

TIP

Preparing a cooked pudding and pie filling with extra milk makes a wonderfully easy sauce. Try vanilla pudding for a quick custard sauce.

VARIATION

Replace the chocolate with vanilla pudding and pie filling. The flavor is not as chocolatey, but it is still delicious.

---

1. Prepare and bake cake according to package directions for 13-by 9-inch (3.5 L) cake. Cool completely. Cut into 1-inch (2.5 cm) cubes.

2. In a large saucepan, combine pudding mix and milk. Cook, stirring constantly, over medium heat until mixture comes to a boil. Cover surface of pudding with plastic wrap and cool completely.

3. *Assembly:* Put 1/4 cup (50 mL) pie filling on bottom of trifle bowl or large glass serving bowl. Drizzle 2 tbsp (25 mL) of the liqueur on top. Place half of cake cubes on filling. Sprinkle with half of remaining liqueur. Cover with half of pie filling. Pour half of pudding over filling. Repeat layers with remaining ingredients. Beat cream to stiff peaks. Spread over top of pudding layer. Garnish with cherries and shaved chocolate. Chill until serving. Store leftover trifle in refrigerator.

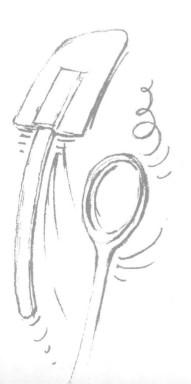

Death by Chocolate

Preheat oven to 350° F (180° C)
Two 8-inch (1.2 L) or 9-inch (1.5L) round cake pans, greased and floured
Trifle bowl or large glass serving bowl

Serves 12 to 16

1	pkg (18.25 oz [515 g]) dark-chocolate cake mix	1
1	pkg (4-serving size) chocolate mousse dessert mix, prepared	1
2 cups	whipping (35%) cream	500 mL
2 tbsp	liqueur (such as Amaretto or Kahlua)	25 mL
4	crisp toffee chocolate bars such as Skor (each 1.4 oz [39 g]), crushed	4

This is definitely the dessert to die for. It is a chocoholic's dream come true.

1. Prepare and bake cake according to package directions to make two round layers. Cool 10 minutes in pans on a wire rack, then remove layers and cool completely. Reserve 1 layer for another use and cut other layer with a long, sharp knife into 1-inch (2.5 cm) cubes.

2. Prepare mousse mix according to package directions. Beat cream to stiff peaks.

3. Put half the cake cubes in trifle bowl. Drizzle half the liqueur on top. Spread half the mousse, then half the whipped cream on top. Sprinkle half the chocolate bars over cream. Repeat layering with remaining ingredients. Cover bowl with plastic wrap and chill for at least 4 hours before serving. Store leftover dessert in refrigerator.

TIP

Prepare the cake ahead and freeze. Cut into cubes while still semi-frozen.

To crush chocolate bars, chill them first then pound them right in the package using an unbreakable utensil such as the back of a wooden spoon, a rolling pin or a hammer.

Use any liqueur that you like and goes well with chocolate, such as Amaretto, Kahlua, Tia Maria or Crème de Cacao.

For a more "cakey" dessert, use both cake layers.

VARIATION

If you can't find Skor bars, try any crisp toffee chocolate bar.

CHEESECAKES

Lemon Glazed Cheesecake Squares

Preheat oven to 350° F (180° C)
13- by 9-inch (3.5 L) cake pan, greased

Serves 12 to 16

If you like lemon you'll love this dessert – light and creamy with a great lemon taste. Cut into bite-size pieces for a cookie tray or into larger pieces for a dessert.

TIP

For best flavor (and convenience), prepare a day ahead. Line pan completely with aluminum foil or parchment paper. You can then remove the cooled cake for easy slicing.

VARIATION

Add 1/2 cup (125 mL) ground nuts to the crust.

For a stronger lemon taste, try making the crust with a lemon cake mix.

Crust		
1	pkg (18.25 oz [515 g]) white cake mix	1
1/2 cup	butter, melted	125 mL
Filling		
1 1/2 lbs	cream cheese, softened	750 g
3/4 cup	granulated sugar	175 mL
3	eggs	3
1/3 cup	lemon juice	75 mL
Topping		
2 cups	sour cream	500 mL
3 tbsp	granulated sugar	45 mL
Glaze		
1/2 cup	granulated sugar	125 mL
2 tbsp	cornstarch	25 mL
3/4 cup	water	175 mL
1/3 cup	lemon juice	75 mL
1	egg yolk, beaten	1
1 tbsp	butter	15 mL

1. *Crust:* Combine cake mix and melted butter; stir together until well blended. Press firmly into prepared pan. Bake 15 to 20 minutes, or until light golden.

2. *Filling:* In a large mixer bowl, beat cream cheese and sugar on high speed until smooth. Add eggs, one at a time, and lemon juice, beating until smooth. Spread over crust. Bake 35 to 40 minutes or just until set in center.

3. *Topping:* Combine sour cream and sugar. Spread over hot cheesecake. Return to oven and bake 5 minutes longer. Cool 1 hour on wire rack.

4. *Glaze:* Prepare glaze while cheesecake is cooling. In a small saucepan, combine sugar and cornstarch. Stir in water, lemon juice and egg yolk. Cook over medium heat, stirring constantly, until mixture comes to a boil and thickens. Add butter, stirring until melted. Cool slightly. Spread evenly over cheesecake. Chill until serving. Store leftover cheesecake in refrigerator.

Chocolate Marble Cheesecake

Preheat oven to 350° F (180° C)
10-inch (25 cm) springform pan

Serves 12 to 16

The marbling of light and dark batters on a dark crust is stunning.

Crust

1	pkg (18.25 oz [515 g]) devil's food cake mix	1
1/2 cup	butter, melted	125 mL

Filling

1 1/2 lbs	cream cheese, softened	750 g
3/4 cup	granulated sugar	175 mL
3	eggs	3
1	square (1 oz [28 g]) unsweetened chocolate, melted	1

1. *Crust:* Combine cake mix and melted butter. Stir together until well blended. Press evenly on bottom of pan. Bake 10 minutes. Remove from oven. Cool while preparing filling. Increase oven temperature to 450° F (230° C).

2. *Filling:* In a large mixer bowl, beat cream cheese and sugar on medium speed until smooth. Add eggs, one at a time, beating well after each addition. Remove 1 cup (250 mL) filling; stir in melted chocolate. Spread plain filling over crust. Drop spoonfuls of chocolate filling on top. Run knife through batters to create marbling effect. Bake for 7 minutes, then reduce temperature to 250° F (120° C) and bake 30 minutes longer or just until set. Run knife around edge of pan to loosen cake. Cool completely on a wire rack. Chill until serving. Store leftover cheesecake in refrigerator.

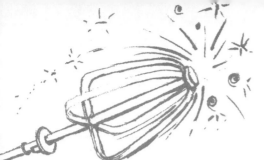

Pumpkin Cheesecake

Preheat oven to 350° F (180° C)
10-inch (25 cm) springform pan

Serves 12 to 16

Tired of traditional pumpkin pie during the holiday season? Even pumpkin-haters will love this dessert.

TIP

Be sure to use pumpkin purée – not pumpkin pie filling, which has sugar and spices added to it.

Don't be alarmed if the cake puffs up while baking – it will settle on cooling.

Replace pumpkin pie spice with 2 tsp (10 mL) ground cinnamon, and 1/4 to 1/2 tsp (1 to 2 mL) each ground nutmeg and ground cloves.

VARIATION

Bake cheesecake in a 13- by 9-inch (3.5 L) pan at 350° F (180° C) for 30 to 35 minutes. You can cut this into large dessert pieces or small cookie-tray-sized treats.

Crust

1	pkg (18.25 oz [515 g]) spice cake mix	1
1/2 cup	butter, melted	125 mL

Filling

1 1/2 lbs	cream cheese, softened	750 g
1	can (14 oz [398 mL]) sweetened condensed milk	1
1	can (14 oz [398 mL]) pumpkin purée (not pie filling)	1
4	eggs	4
1 tbsp	pumpkin pie spice	15 mL

Topping

1 1/2 cups	whipping (35%) cream	375 mL
1/4 cup	confectioner's (icing) sugar, sifted	50 mL
1/4 cup	sliced almonds, toasted	50 mL

1. *Crust:* Combine cake mix and melted butter. Mix well. Press firmly on bottom of pan. Set aside.

2. *Filling:* In a large mixer bowl, beat cream cheese and sweetened condensed milk on high speed for 2 minutes. Add pumpkin, eggs and spice. Beat for 1 minute longer, or until smooth. Pour over prepared crust. Bake 55 to 60 minutes or just until set. Run knife around edge of pan to loosen cake. Cool completely on a wire rack then chill 2 hours or overnight.

3. *Topping:* Beat cream and confectioner's sugar to stiff peaks. Spread over cheesecake. Sprinkle with toasted almonds. Chill until serving. Store leftover cheesecake in refrigerator.

Plain & Simple Cheesecake

Preheat oven to 325° F (160° C)
13- by 9-inch (3.5 L) cake pan, greased

Serves 12 to 16

Plain cheesecake is very versatile. You can top it with a pie filling, fresh fruit, fruit sauce or enjoy it plain and simple.

TIP

Cheesecakes can be refrigerated 1 week or frozen for up to 2 months. Thaw overnight in refrigerator before serving.

Cheesecakes are best prepared a day ahead to let flavor and texture mellow.

VARIATION

You may prefer a yellow cake mix for a more "graham cracker" crust taste.

Crust

1	pkg (18.25 oz [515 g]) white cake mix	1
1/3 cup	butter, melted	75 mL
1	egg	1

Filling

1 lb	cream cheese, softened	500 g
1	can (14 oz [398 mL]) sweetened condensed milk	1
3	eggs	3
1/2 cup	sour cream	125 mL
1/2 cup	reserved cake mix (from above)	125 mL
2 tbsp	lemon juice	25 mL
1 tsp	grated lemon zest	5 mL

Topping

2 cups	sour cream	500 mL
1/4 cup	granulated sugar	50 mL
1 tsp	vanilla extract	5 mL

1. *Crust:* Measure out 1/2 cup (125 mL) of the cake mix. Reserve for filling. In a large mixer bowl, combine remaining cake mix, melted butter and egg. Beat on low speed for 1 minute or until a soft, smooth dough forms. Pat evenly over bottom and 1 inch (2.5 cm) up sides of prepared pan.

Recipe continues....

CRANBERRY BANANA LOAF (PAGE 90) ➤
OVERLEAF: FRUIT-TOPPED MINI CHEESECAKES (PAGE 132)

2. *Filling:* In a large mixer bowl, beat cream cheese and sweetened condensed milk on medium speed just to blend. Add eggs, one at a time, beating lightly after each until smooth. Add sour cream, reserved cake mix, lemon juice and zest. Beat on medium speed for 1 minute. Spread evenly on crust. Bake 30 to 35 minutes or just until set.

3. *Topping:* Combine sour cream, sugar and vanilla. Spread evenly over hot cheesecake. Return to oven and bake 5 to 7 minutes longer or until topping is set. Run knife around edge of pan to loosen cake. Cool completely on wire rack. Refrigerate overnight to let flavors mellow. Store leftover cheesecake in refrigerator.

≺ PEACH COBBLER (PAGE 117)

130

Chocolate Toffee Crunch Cheesecake

Preheat oven to 325° F (160° C)
13- by 9-inch (3.5 L) cake pan, greased

Serves 12 to 16

The combination of crunchy caramel on top, a rich creamy chocolate cheesecake filling and decadent chocolate base is a real winner.

TIP

Turn bottom of springform pan over before filling so the lip side is down. With no lip to contend with, cutting is easy.

Cut cheesecakes with a long, sharp knife dipped in hot water and wiped off between each slice.

VARIATION

Omit melted chocolate in filling if desired.

Crust

1	pkg (18.25 oz [515 g]) devil's food cake mix	1
1/3 cup	butter, melted	75 mL
1	egg	1

Filling

1 lb	cream cheese, softened	500 g
1	can (14 oz [398 mL]) sweetened condensed milk	1
2	squares (each 1 oz [28 g]) semi-sweet chocolate, melted and cooled	2
3	eggs	3
1/2 cup	sour cream	125 mL
1/2 cup	reserved cake mix (from above)	125 mL
1 1/3 cups	crunchy toffee bits	325 mL

1. *Crust:* Measure out 1/2 cup (125 mL) of the cake mix. Reserve for filling. In a large mixer bowl, combine remaining cake mix, melted butter and egg. Beat on low speed for 1 minute or until a soft, smooth dough forms. Pat evenly over bottom and 1 inch (2.5 cm) up sides of prepared pan.

◆ 2. *Filling:* In a large mixer bowl, beat cream cheese, sweetened condensed milk and melted chocolate on medium speed just to blend. Add eggs, one at a time, beating lightly after each until smooth. Add sour cream and reserved cake mix. Beat on medium speed for 1 minute. Stir in 1 cup (250 mL) of the toffee bits. Spread evenly on crust. Sprinkle remaining 1/3 cup (75 mL) toffee bits on top. Bake 45 to 50 minutes or just until set. Run knife around edge of pan to loosen cake. Cool completely on wire rack. Refrigerate overnight to let flavors mellow. Store leftover cheesecake in refrigerator.

Fruit-Topped Mini Cheesecakes

Preheat oven to 350° F (180° C)
24 muffin cups lined with large paper cup liners or greased

Serves 24

A perfect make-ahead dessert for your next party. Top with a variety of fruit pie fillings or fresh fruit for an attractive presentation. A fresh mint leaf is a pretty finishing touch.

TIP

Buy deep paper cup liners if possible. While paper liners make storage and transportation easy, you can also bake these cheesecakes in greased muffin cups with no liners if using within a day.

For another attractive presentation, omit sour cream layer. Place cheesecakes upside down on plate and serve with fresh fruit sauce.

Crust

1	pkg (18.25 oz [515 g]) white cake mix	1
1/3 cup	butter, melted	75 mL

Filling

1 lb	cream cheese, softened	500 g
3/4 cup	granulated sugar	175 mL
3	eggs	3
1 tsp	vanilla extract	5 mL

Topping

2 cups	sour cream	500 mL
1/3 cup	granulated sugar	75 mL
	Fruit pie filling or fresh fruit	

1. *Crust:* In a large mixer bowl, combine cake mix and melted butter. Beat on low speed for 2 minutes or until crumble mixture is thoroughly blended. Divide mixture evenly in muffin cups. Press down firmly with back of a spoon.

2. *Filling:* Beat cream cheese and sugar together on low speed until blended. Add eggs, one at a time, then vanilla, beating until smooth. Spoon into prepared cups, dividing evenly. Bake 20 to 25 minutes or until set.

3. *Topping:* Combine sour cream and sugar. Spoon over hot baked cheesecakes, spreading to cover tops. Return to oven and bake 5 minutes longer. Cool completely in pan on a wire rack.

4. To serve, carefully remove paper cups and top cheesecakes with a spoonful of pie filling or a small piece of fruit such as a mandarin, raspberry, strawberry or kiwi. Store leftover cheesecakes in refrigerator.

COOKIES

134

Chocolate Macadamia Nut Oatmeal Cookies

Preheat oven to 375° F (190° C)
Baking sheets, greased

Makes about 5 dozen cookies

TIP

Use large-flake oats for a more "oaty" taste. Be sure not to use instant oatmeal.

VARIATION

Try substituting pecans for macadamia nuts and white chocolate chunks for semi-sweet.

1	pkg (18.25 oz [515 g]) white cake mix	1
1/2 cup	quick-cooking oats	125 mL
1/2 cup	butter, melted	125 mL
2	eggs	2
1 tsp	vanilla extract	5 mL
1 1/2 cups	coarsely chopped macadamia nuts	375 mL
1 1/2 cups	semi-sweet chocolate chunks or chips	375 mL

1. In a large mixer bowl, combine cake mix, oats, melted butter, eggs and vanilla. Beat on low speed for 1 minute or just until smooth. Stir in nuts and chocolate chunks.

2. Drop dough by rounded tablespoonfuls onto prepared sheets. Bake 10 to 15 minutes or until light golden. Cool 1 minute on wire racks or until firm on baking sheets then remove to racks and cool completely.

Double Chocolate Dreams

Preheat oven to 375° F (190° C)
Baking sheets, greased

Makes about 4 dozen cookies

A chocoholic's dream. Try them warm from the oven, but be prepared to make a second batch.

1	pkg (18.25 oz [515 g]) devil's food cake mix	1
2	eggs	2
1/2 cup	vegetable oil	125 mL
2 cups	semi-sweet chocolate chips	500 mL
3/4 cup	chopped nuts	175 mL

1. In a large mixer bowl, combine cake mix, eggs and oil. With a wooden spoon or on low speed of mixer, mix for 1 minute or until well blended. Dough will be stiff. Stir in chocolate chips and nuts.

2. Drop dough by rounded tablespoonfuls onto prepared baking sheets. Bake 8 to 12 minutes or just until set. Cool 1 minute on baking sheet on a wire rack, then transfer cookies to rack and cool completely.

TIP

A small ice cream scoop with wire release (about 3/4 oz [35 mL]) is ideal for spooning out the dough. You get nicely shaped cookies of uniform size.

VARIATION

Use yellow cake mix for a traditional chocolate chip cookie look.

Replace nuts with 1 cup (250 mL) coconut.

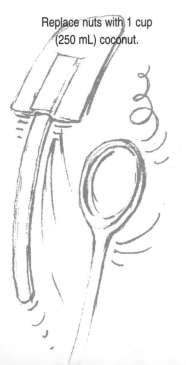

Gingerbread People

Preheat oven to 375° F (190° C)
Baking sheets, greased

**Makes about 2 dozen
(4-inch [10 cm]) cookies**

Don't limit these to the festive season. With different cookie-cutter shapes and decorations, you can make them a year-round treat.

1	pkg (18.25 oz [515 g]) spice cake mix	1
3/4 cup	all-purpose flour	175 mL
2 tsp	ground ginger	10 mL
2	eggs	2
1/3 cup	vegetable oil	75 mL
1/3 cup	molasses	75 mL
	Raisins for eyes (optional)	
	Vanilla icing	
	Colorful candies	

TIP

You can omit raisins and decorate later with icing. If baking ahead, don't put on the raisin decorations. Cool and store cookies in container with loose-fitting lid. They are ready to decorate when you are.

VARIATION

Different sizes of gingerbread people cutters are available. Decrease baking time for smaller people and increase time for larger ones.

1. In a large bowl, combine cake mix, flour and ginger. Add eggs, oil and molasses. Mix thoroughly with wooden spoon to form a smooth dough (dough will be soft). Chill 2 to 3 hours until firm enough to roll out.

2. Roll dough out on lightly floured surface to 1/4-inch (1 cm) thickness. Cut with 4-inch (10 cm) gingerbread person cookie cutter. Place on prepared baking sheets. Press raisins in dough for eyes and buttons, if desired. Bake 8 to 12 minutes or until edges start to brown. Cool 5 minutes or until firm on baking sheet, then remove to racks and cool completely.

3. Decorate if desired with frosting and an assortment of colorful candies.

Rum Balls

Preheat oven to 375° F (190° C)

Makes about 6 dozen cookies

1	pkg (18.25 oz [515 g]) chocolate cake mix, baked and cooled	1
1 cup	finely chopped walnuts or almonds	250 mL
4 tsp	rum	20 mL
2 cups	confectioner's (icing) sugar, sifted	500 mL
1/4 cup	cocoa	50 mL
	Finely chopped nuts or chocolate sprinkles	

There are many recipes for this classic no-bake treat. It's nice to make while another recipe is in the oven – or in the summer, when you don't want to put the oven on.

1. Crumble cake into a large bowl. Stir with fork until crumbs are fine and uniform in size. Add nuts, rum, confectioner's sugar and cocoa. Stir until thoroughly blended. Shape heaping tablespoonfuls of cake mixture into balls. Roll in nuts or chocolate sprinkles, pressing firmly to adhere coating to balls. Place on waxed paper and let set for 1 hour. Store in airtight container in refrigerator.

TIP

An excellent way to use leftover cake, if that ever happens. Keep this recipe in mind if you have the opportunity to bake an extra cake when preparing another cake recipe.

Prepare several days ahead to let flavors develop.

Place in small paper cups to serve or for gift-giving.

VARIATION

Rum can be replaced with 1 tbsp (15 mL) rum extract.

Peanut Butter Cookies

Preheat oven to 375° F (190° C)
Baking sheets, greased

Makes about 4 dozen cookies

1 cup	peanut butter	250 mL
2	eggs	2
1 tbsp	milk	15 mL
1	pkg (18.25 oz [515 g]) white cake mix	1
	Granulated sugar	

An old-fashioned favorite made easier to prepare.

TIP

Be sure to use fresh peanut butter. Because of its high oil content, peanut butter can go rancid quite quickly.

A potato masher works well for pressing a pattern on top of cookies.

For extra-crunchy cookies, use crunchy peanut butter. You may need a bit more to make a soft dough.

VARIATION

Press a chocolate kiss candy or whole peanut on top of cookie for decoration.

1. In a large bowl, combine peanut butter, eggs, milk and half of cake mix. Stir thoroughly to blend. Add remaining cake mix. Blend thoroughly, using hands to form a smooth dough.

2. Shape dough into 1-inch (2.5 cm) balls. Place on prepared baking sheets. Press flat with a fork dipped in sugar. Bake 10 to 12 minutes or until set. Cool 5 minutes or until firm on baking sheet, then remove to racks and cool completely.

Double Chocolate Chewies

Preheat oven to 375° F (190° C)
Baking sheets, greased

**Makes about 4 dozen
cookies**

*A versatile chocolate cookie
that lends itself to a variety
of additions such as chips,
nuts and dried fruit.*

1	pkg (18.25 oz [515 g]) devil's cake mix	1
1	egg	1
1/3 cup	water	75 mL
1/4 cup	butter, melted	50 mL
1 1/2 cups	white chocolate chips	375 mL
1/2 cup	dried cranberries	125 mL
1/2 cup	slivered almonds or pecans	125 mL

1. In a large mixer bowl, combine cake mix, egg, water and melted butter. Beat on low speed for 1 minute or just until smooth. Stir in chocolate chips, cranberries and nuts. Mix well.

2. Drop dough by rounded tablespoonfuls onto prepared baking sheets. Bake 8 to 10 minutes or just until softly set. Cool 1 minute or until firm on baking sheets, then remove to racks and cool completely.

TIP

Don't store crisp cookies and soft cookies together. The crisp ones won't stay that way for long!

Use sheets of waxed paper between layers to prevent cookies from sticking together.

Cookies freeze very well for up to 6 months. They thaw in about 15 minutes.

VARIATION

Substitute cold strong coffee for the water.

Chunky Chocolate Pecan Cookies

Preheat oven to 375° F (190° C)
Baking sheets, greased

Makes about 4 1/2 dozen cookies

A good choice for the cookie jar.

1	pkg (18.25 oz [515 g]) white cake mix	1
1/2 cup	butter, melted	125 mL
2	eggs	2
1 tsp	vanilla extract	5 mL
1 1/2 cups	semi-sweet chocolate chunks or chips	375 mL
1 1/4 cups	coarsely chopped pecans	300 mL

1. In a large mixer bowl, combine cake mix, melted butter, eggs and vanilla. Beat on low speed for 1 minute or just until smooth. Stir in chocolate chips and nuts.

2. Drop dough by rounded tablespoonfuls onto prepared baking sheets. Bake 10 to 15 minutes or until light golden. Cool 1 minute or until firm on baking sheets, then remove to racks and cool completely.

TIP

Make smaller cookies for cookie boxes or cookie trays where there are a variety of items. That way, people can try several different kinds. For lunch boxes, you may prefer larger cookies.

VARIATION

Vary the type of nuts and chocolate to suit your personal taste. Try macadamia nuts and white chocolate chunks.

BARS & SQUARES

Toffee Crunch Bars

Preheat oven to 350° F (180° C)
13- by 9-inch (3.5 L) cake pan, greased

Makes about 3 dozen bars

*Here's a different way
to enjoy your favorite
chocolate bar.*

1	pkg (18.25 oz [515 g]) white cake mix	1
1/3 cup	packed brown sugar	75 mL
2	eggs	2
1/2 cup	butter, melted	125 mL
1 cup	crushed chocolate-coated toffee bars (Skor, Heath, Butterfinger)	250 mL
2/3 cup	chopped almonds	150 mL

1. In a large mixer bowl, combine cake mix, brown sugar, eggs and melted butter. Beat on low speed for 2 minutes or until smooth. Stir in crushed chocolate bar and almonds. Spread batter evenly in prepared pan. Bake 25 to 30 minutes or until golden. Cool completely in pan on a wire rack. Cut into bars.

TIP

Freeze chocolate bars so they become brittle and break up easily without melting.

Buy "misshaped" chocolate bars on sale and keep a supply in the freezer for this recipe.

If the chocolate bar you choose has lots of nuts, decrease the quantity of nuts in the recipe.

VARIATION

Almost any chocolate bar will work. The softer chewy ones will have to be cold to chop.

Replace chocolate bars with toffee bits and chocolate chips.

Chocolate Raspberry Almond Oat Bars

Preheat oven to 375° F (190° C)
13- by 9-inch (3.5 L) cake pan, greased

Makes about 3 dozen bars

The best of both worlds – healthy oats and decadent chocolate chips.

1	pkg (18.25 oz [515 g]) white cake mix	1
2 1/2 cups	quick-cooking oats	625 mL
1 cup	butter, melted	250 mL
1 cup	seedless raspberry jam	250 mL
1 1/3 cups	semi-sweet chocolate chips	325 mL
3/4 cup	chopped almonds or pecans	175 mL
	Confectioner's (icing) sugar (optional)	

TIP

Stir jam to soften for easy spreading.

Spread jam over base, leaving a 1/2-inch (1 cm) border. This prevents jam from sticking to side of pan.

Regular raspberry jam works fine, although the seedless variety has a more intense flavor.

VARIATION

Replace raspberry jam with apricot. It's not as pretty but it tastes good.

1. In a large bowl, combine cake mix, oats and melted butter, mixing until well blended. Press half of crumbles (3 cups [750 mL]) firmly into prepared pan. Spread jam evenly over unbaked crust. Sprinkle chocolate chips over jam. Stir almonds into remaining crumble mixture. Sprinkle evenly over chips. Bake 35 to 40 minutes or until golden. Cool completely in pan on a wire rack. Cut into bars.

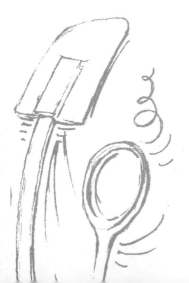

Lots of Lemon Squares

Preheat oven to 350° F (180° C)
13- by 9-inch (3.5 L) cake pan, greased

Makes about 4 dozen squares

A hazelnut cookie base with tart, lemony topping. These squares make a refreshing complement to decadent chocolate delights.

TIP	

Toast hazelnuts for the best flavor. There's no need to remove the skins. They add a wonderfully nutty color and flavor.

A sprinkling of confectioner's sugar before serving makes a nice finishing touch.

VARIATION	

Replace hazelnuts with unblanched almonds.

Crust		
1	pkg (18.25 oz [515 g]) lemon cake mix	1
1/2 cup	finely chopped hazelnuts	125 mL
1/2 cup	butter, melted	125 mL
Topping		
4	eggs	4
2 cups	granulated sugar	500 mL
1/3 cup	lemon juice	75 mL
1/4 cup	all-purpose flour	50 mL
1 tsp	baking powder	5 mL
1 tsp	grated lemon zest	5 mL
	Confectioner's (icing) sugar (optional)	

1. *Crust:* In a large bowl, combine cake mix, hazelnuts and melted butter, mixing until well blended. Press firmly into prepared pan. Bake 12 minutes or until light golden.

2. *Topping:* In a small bowl, whisk together eggs, sugar and lemon juice until blended. Add flour, baking powder and zest. Mix well. Pour over hot crust. Bake 20 to 25 minutes longer or until set and light golden. Cool completely in pan on a wire rack. Dust with confectioner's sugar before serving, if desired. Cut into squares.

Chunky Butterscotch Nut Squares

Preheat oven to 350° F (180° C)
13- by 9-inch (3.5 L) cake pan, greased

Makes about 4 dozen squares

Made-to-order for nut fans.

Crust

1	pkg (18.25 oz [515 g]) yellow cake mix	1
2/3 cup	butter, melted	150 mL

Topping

1 2/3 cups	butterscotch chips (1 pkg [10 oz/300g])	400 mL
3/4 cup	corn syrup	175 mL
3 tbsp	butter	45 mL
2 cups	salted mixed nuts	500 mL

1. *Crust:* In a large bowl, combine cake mix and melted butter, mixing until well blended. Press firmly into prepared pan. Bake 25 to 30 minutes or until golden. Cool completely in pan on a wire rack.

2. *Topping:* In a saucepan over low heat, combine butterscotch chips, corn syrup and butter, stirring often until smoothly melted. Cool slightly. Spread over cooled base. Scatter nuts evenly over top. Press gently into topping. Chill 1 hour or until firm for easy slicing. Cut into squares.

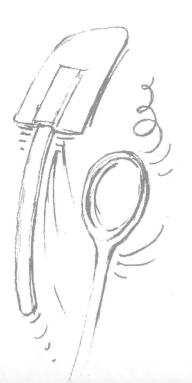

Chocolate Cherry Bars

Preheat oven to 350° F (180° C)
17 1/2- by 11 1/2-inch (3 L) jelly roll pan, greased

Makes about 5 dozen bars

1	pkg (6-serving size) chocolate pudding and pie filling (not instant)	1
1	pkg (18.25 oz [515 g]) chocolate cake mix	1
1 cup	chopped maraschino cherries	250 mL
1 cup	semi-sweet chocolate chips	250 mL
3/4 cup	chopped nuts	175 mL

These bars have an unusual taste and texture. They're moist and cake-like with an attractive shiny top. Serve with whipped cream for dessert.

1. Cook pudding according to package directions. Remove 1 cup (250 mL) for another use – or simply enjoy eating it now! In a large mixer bowl, combine remaining warm pudding and cake mix. Beat on low speed or by hand for 1 minute or until smooth. Stir in cherries. Spread evenly in prepared pan. Sprinkle with chocolate chips and nuts. Bake 20 to 25 minutes or until set. Cool completely on a wire rack. Cut into bars.

TIP

Be sure to prepare the pudding just when you're going to make these bars, not ahead of time. It should be warm.

VARIATION

Vary the topping. It's great with a combination of white, milk and semi-sweet chocolate chips.

Omit nuts and increase chips to 2 cups (500 mL).

Caramel Filled Brownies

Preheat oven to 350° F (180° C)
13- by 9-inch (3.5 L) cake pan, greased

**Makes about 4 dozen
squares**

*There are many varieties
of bars that taste like
chocolate caramel candies,
but this is one of my
favorites (based on many
taste comparisons!).*

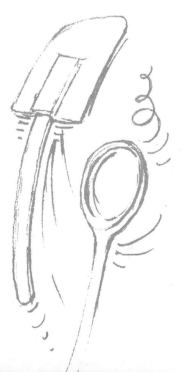

TIP

Chill caramels for easier
unwrapping. It's still a fussy job,
but easily forgotten when you
taste the squares.

VARIATION

Try using chocolate caramels.
It doesn't look as attractive, but
real chocoholics won't care!

Filling

14 oz	caramels, unwrapped (about 50 caramels)	425 g
1/2 cup	evaporated milk	125 mL

Base & Topping

1	pkg (18.25 oz [515 g]) devil's food cake mix	1
1 cup	chopped pecans	250 mL
1/2 cup	butter, softened	125 mL
1/2 cup	evaporated milk	125 mL
1 cup	semi-sweet chocolate chips	250 mL

1. *Filling:* In a saucepan combine caramels and evaporated milk. Cook over low heat, stirring often, until smoothly melted. Keep warm while preparing brownie batter.

2. *Base & Topping:* In a mixer bowl, combine cake mix and pecans. Cut in butter with a pastry blender or a fork until crumbly. Add evaporated milk. Mix well. Batter will be thick. Spread half of batter in prepared pan. Bake 12 to 15 minutes or until set. Remove from oven. Sprinkle chocolate chips on top. Drizzle caramel sauce over chips. Spread carefully to cover base. Drop remaining batter by spoonfuls over caramel. Bake 15 to 20 minutes longer or just until set. Brownies will firm up on cooling. Cool completely in pan on a wire rack. Cut into squares.

Chocolate Nut Bars

Preheat oven to 350° F (180° C)
15 1/2- by 10 1/2-inch (2 L) jelly roll pan, greased

Makes about 5 dozen bars

The large pan goes a long way. Think of this easy-to-make treat when you've got a crowd coming or for your next family reunion.

1. In a large mixer bowl, combine cake mix, brown sugar, eggs, water and butter. Beat on low speed for 1 minute or just until blended. Stir in nuts. Spread evenly in prepared pan. Bake 15 to 20 minutes or just until set. Cool completely in pan on a wire rack. Spread chocolate frosting evenly over bars. Cut into bars.

TIP

Line the pan with greased parchment or aluminum foil for easy removal and clean up.

These freeze very well. In fact, they are good frozen. Wrap and freeze some individually, then remove to pack into lunches as needed.

VARIATION

For a mocha taste, dissolve 1 tbsp (15 mL) instant coffee in the water of the batter. Frost with a mocha butter frosting.

Cranberry Chip Bars

Preheat oven to 350° F (180° C)
13- by 9-inch (3.5 L) cake pan, greased

Makes about 4 dozen bars

Creamy white chocolate, crunchy nuts and tart cranberries combine in this colorful, festive bar.

1	pkg (18.25 oz [515 g]) white cake mix	1
1/4 cup	packed brown sugar	50 mL
2	eggs	2
1/4 cup	butter, softened	50 mL
1/4 cup	water	50 mL
1 cup	dried cranberries	250 mL
1 cup	white chocolate chips	250 mL
1 cup	chopped almonds	250 mL

1. In a large mixer bowl, combine cake mix, brown sugar, eggs, butter and water. Beat on low speed for 1 minute or until smooth. Stir in cranberries, chips and nuts. Spread batter evenly in prepared pan. Bake 25 to 30 minutes or until set and light golden. Cool completely in pan on a wire rack. Cut into bars.

TIP

Check for doneness at the minimum time recommended. Ovens are often hot and dark pans bake contents faster. You can always bake it longer rather than being disappointed with an overdone item.

It's a good idea to keep a reliable oven thermometer in your oven as a check on the temperature.

For a sweeter bar, top with a lemon glaze or frosting.

VARIATION

Replace almonds with pecans or walnuts and cranberries with chopped dried apricots.

Chewy Cherry Bars

Preheat oven to 350° F (180° C)
13- by 9-inch (3.5 L) cake pan, greased

Makes about 4 dozen bars

A colorful addition to your Christmas cookie tray. You'll never go wrong with extras in the freezer.

TIP

If you're counting calories during the holiday season, omit the frosting.

Chill bars for easy cutting and storing.

VARIATION

Replace each 1/2 tsp (2 mL) almond extract with 1 tbsp (15 mL) lemon juice in the filling and frosting.

Crust		
1	pkg (18.25 oz [515 g]) white cake mix	1
3/4 cup	butter, softened	175 mL
Filling		
2	eggs	2
1 cup	packed brown sugar	250 mL
1/2 tsp	almond extract	2 mL
2 tbsp	all-purpose flour	25 mL
1 tsp	baking powder	5 mL
1 cup	flaked coconut	250 mL
1 cup	chopped drained maraschino cherries	250 mL
1/2 cup	chopped pecans or walnuts	125 mL
Frosting		
1/4 cup	butter, softened	50 mL
1/2 tsp	almond extract	2 mL
2 cups	confectioner's (icing) sugar, sifted	500 mL
3 to 4 tbsp	light (10%) cream	45 to 60 mL

1. *Crust:* In a large mixer bowl, combine cake mix and butter. Beat on low speed until well blended. Press firmly into prepared pan. Bake 10 to 12 minutes or until light golden.

2. *Filling:* In a large mixer bowl, beat eggs, brown sugar and extract together until smoothly blended. Stir in flour and baking powder. Mix well. Stir in coconut, cherries and nuts. Spread evenly over warm crust. Bake 25 to 30 minutes longer or until set and golden. Cool completely in pan on a wire rack.

3. *Frosting:* In a small mixer bowl, beat butter and almond extract until smooth. Gradually add confectioner's sugar and cream, beating on medium speed until smooth and creamy. Spread over cooled bars. Chill until frosting is firm. Cut into bars.

Caramel Pecan Bars

Preheat oven to 350° F (180° C)
17 1/2- by 11 1/2-inch (3 L) jelly roll pan, greased

Makes about 5 dozen bars

These look fabulous and taste even better. Bet your tasters they can't eat just one!

TIP

To ensure crust is evenly distributed, put blobs of dough evenly over pan, then press out with heel of hand to cover pan.

Do not substitute margarine for butter.

VARIATION

Replace white cake mix with yellow.

Crust

1	pkg (18.25 oz [515 g]) white cake mix	1
3/4 cup	butter, melted	175 mL

Topping

3 1/2 cups	pecan halves	875 mL
3/4 cup	butter	175 mL
1/2 cup	liquid honey	125 mL
3/4 cup	packed brown sugar	175 mL
1/4 cup	whipping (35%) cream	50 mL

1. *Crust:* Combine cake mix and melted butter, mixing until well blended. Press firmly into prepared pan. Bake 15 minutes or until light golden. Cool 5 minutes on a wire rack.

2. *Topping:* Scatter pecans evenly over crust. For the most attractive appearance, turn rounded-side up. In a large, heavy saucepan, melt butter and honey. Add brown sugar. Boil 5 to 7 minutes, stirring constantly, until mixture is thickened and a rich caramel color. Remove from heat. Carefully stir in cream. Mix well and pour evenly over pecans. Bake 15 minutes longer or just until topping is bubbling around sides of pan. Cool completely in pan on a wire rack. Cut into bars.

Strawberry Cheesecake Squares

Preheat oven to 350° F (180° C)
13- by 9-inch (3.5 L) cake pan, greased

**Makes about 3 dozen
squares**

*Cut these into large squares
for a dessert or bite-size for
a cookie tray.*

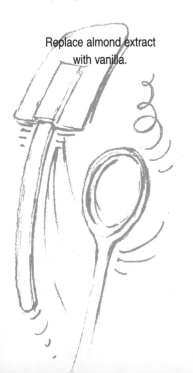

Crust

1	pkg (18.25 oz [515 g]) white cake mix	1
3/4 cup	finely chopped almonds	175 mL
3/4 cup	butter	175 mL

Filling

1 lb	cream cheese, softened	500 g
2/3 cup	granulated sugar	150 mL
2	eggs	2
1/2 tsp	almond extract	2 mL
1 cup	strawberry jam	250 mL
3/4 cup	sliced almonds	175 mL

1. *Crust:* In a large bowl, combine cake mix and chopped almonds. With a pastry blender or two knives, cut in butter until crumbly. Reserve 1 cup (250 mL) for topping. Press remainder into prepared pan. Bake 15 minutes or until light golden.

2. *Filling:* In a large mixer bowl, beat cream cheese, sugar, eggs and extract together on medium speed until smooth and creamy. Spread evenly over hot crust. Bake 15 minutes longer. Cool 10 minutes on a wire rack. Stir jam until smooth. Spread evenly over filling. Stir sliced almonds into reserved crumble mixture. Sprinkle over jam. Bake 15 minutes longer. Cool completely in pan on a wire rack. Chill 3 hours or overnight before cutting into squares. Store leftover squares in refrigerator.

Lemon Layered Bars

Preheat oven to 350° F (180° C)
13- by 9-inch (3.5 L) cake pan, greased

Makes about 4 dozen bars

Lots of lemon in the crust, filling and crumble topping.

TIP

Cool bar completely, then cut into bars and freeze in small packages. Simply remove the number of bars required. They defrost quickly and there's no need to cut.

VARIATION

Replace lemon zest and juice with lime zest and juice.

Crust

1	pkg (18.25 oz [515 g]) lemon cake mix	1
1	egg	1
1/3 cup	butter, melted	75 mL

Filling

2	eggs	2
2/3 cup	granulated sugar	150 mL
1/3 cup	lemon juice	75 mL
2 tsp	grated lemon zest	10 mL
1/2 tsp	baking powder	2 mL
1/4 tsp	salt	1 mL

Confectioner's (icing) sugar (optional)

1. *Crust:* In a large mixer bowl, combine cake mix, egg and melted butter. Beat on low speed until well blended and crumbly. Reserve 1 cup (250 mL) crumbs for topping. Press remaining crumbs firmly in prepared pan. Bake 12 to 15 minutes or until light golden.

2. *Filling:* In a small mixer bowl, combine eggs, sugar, lemon juice, zest, baking powder and salt. Beat on medium speed until light and foamy. Pour over warm crust. Sprinkle reserved crumble mixture evenly on top. Bake 15 to 20 minutes longer or until set and golden. Cool completely in pan on a wire rack. Dust with confectioner's sugar before serving, if desired. Cut into bars.

Cranberry Pecan Bars

Preheat oven to 350° F (180° C)
13-by 9-inch (3.5 L) cake pan, greased

Makes about 4 dozen bars

A combination of sweet pecan pie and tart cranberries in an easy-to-eat, bite-sized bar.

TIP

The crust will puff slightly during baking but settles down again on cooling.

VARIATION

Replace dried cranberries with chocolate chips.

Crust

1	pkg (18.25 oz [515 g]) white cake mix	1
1/2 cup	butter, melted	125 mL

Topping

4	eggs	4
1 cup	granulated sugar	250 mL
1 cup	corn syrup	250 mL
3 tbsp	butter, melted	45 mL
1 1/2 cups	coarsely chopped pecans	375 mL
3/4 cup	dried cranberries	175 mL

1. *Crust:* In a large bowl, combine cake mix and melted butter, mixing until well blended. Press firmly into prepared pan. Bake 15 minutes or until light golden. Cool 5 minutes on a wire rack before topping.

2. *Topping:* In a medium bowl, beat eggs, sugar, syrup and melted butter together until blended. Stir in pecans and cranberries. Pour evenly over crust. Bake 35 to 40 minutes longer or until set and golden. Cool completely in pan on rack. Cut into bars.

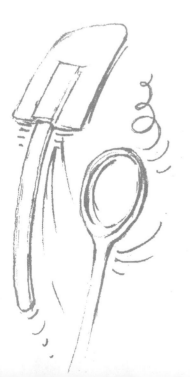

Raspberry Dream Bars

Preheat oven to 350° F (180° C)
13- by 9-inch (3.5 L) cake pan, greased

Makes about 4 dozen bars

*Raspberry and coconut
are a natural flavor
combination.*

TIP

Buy good quality jams. They
have the best flavor and a softer
consistency that is excellent
for spreading.

I prefer the flavor of golden
brown sugar. The dark variety
works well in recipes but
seems to mask delicate flavors
such as raspberry.

Crust		
1	pkg (18.25 oz [515 g]) white cake mix	1
3/4 cup	butter, melted	175 mL
Topping		
2/3 cup	raspberry jam	150 mL
2 1/4 cups	packed brown sugar	550 mL
1/4 cup	all-purpose flour	50 mL
1 1/2 tsp	baking powder	7 mL
1/4 tsp	salt	1 mL
3	eggs	3
1 tbsp	lemon juice	15 mL
3/4 cup	chopped walnuts	175 mL
3/4 cup	shredded or flaked coconut	175 mL

1. *Crust:* In a large bowl, combine cake mix and melted butter, mixing until well blended. Press firmly into prepared pan. Bake 12 to 15 minutes or until light golden. Cool 10 minutes on a wire rack.

2. *Topping:* Spread jam carefully over warm crust. In a large bowl, combine brown sugar, flour, baking powder and salt. Add eggs and lemon juice, mixing until smooth. Stir in nuts and coconut. Spread evenly over jam. Bake 20 to 25 minutes longer or until set and golden. Cool completely in pan on rack. Cut into bars.

Butterscotch Nut Bars

Preheat oven to 350° F (180° C)
13- by 9-inch (3.5 L) cake pan, greased

Makes about 3 dozen bars

A versatile bar that is also great cut into larger squares and served warm with ice cream for dessert.

Crust

1	pkg (18.25 oz [515 g]) white cake mix	1
2/3 cup	butter, melted	150 mL

Topping

4	eggs	4
1 cup	granulated sugar	250 mL
1 cup	corn syrup	250 mL
1/4 cup	butter, melted	50 mL
1 2/3 cups	butterscotch chips (1 pkg [10 oz/300 g])	400 mL
1 1/2 cups	coarsely chopped pecans	375 mL

1. *Crust:* In a large bowl, combine cake mix and melted butter, mixing until well blended. Press firmly into prepared pan. Bake 15 minutes or until light golden.

2. *Topping:* In a medium bowl, whisk eggs just to blend. Add sugar, syrup and melted butter, whisking until smooth. Stir in chips and nuts. Pour over warm crust. Bake 30 to 35 minutes longer or until set and golden. Cool completely in pan on a wire rack. Cut into bars.

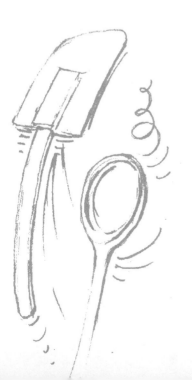

Peanut Butter Chocolate Squares

Preheat oven to 350° F (180° C)
13- by 9-inch (3.5 L) cake pan, greased

Makes about 3 dozen squares

Just like salted peanuts, these squares can quickly become addictive.

Filling

1 2/3 cups	peanut butter chips (1 pkg [10 oz/300 g])	400 mL
1	can (14 oz [398 mL]) sweetened condensed milk	1
2 tbsp	butter	25 mL

Top & Bottom Layer

1	pkg (18.25 oz [515 g]) Swiss chocolate cake mix	1
2/3 cup	butter, softened	150 mL
1/2 cup	milk	125 mL
3/4 cup	chopped peanuts	175 mL
2/3 cup	quick-cooking oats	150 mL

1. *Filling:* In a saucepan combine chips, sweetened condensed milk and butter. Heat, stirring occasionally, over low heat until smoothly melted. Set aside while preparing chocolate mixture.

2. *Top & Bottom Layer:* In a large mixer bowl, combine cake mix, butter and milk. Beat on low speed for 2 minutes or until smooth. Batter will be thick. Stir in peanuts and oats. Spread half the batter in prepared pan. Spread filling over top. Drop remaining chocolate batter by small spoonfuls over filling. Spread carefully to cover filling as much as possible. Bake 30 to 35 minutes or until softly set. Squares will firm up on cooling. Cool completely in pan on a wire rack. Cut into squares.

FROSTINGS, FILLINGS & GLAZES

Basic Frosting Yields

For many of the cake recipes in this book I have recommended one or two frostings that I think complement the cake well. However, this is entirely personal and everyone has his or her own favorites. Here's a guide to the approximate amount of frosting you'll need to cover your cake, so that you can create different combinations without the frustration of not enough frosting. If in doubt, it's always better to have a bit too much than not enough!

Cake size	Frosting required (approx)
13- by 9-inch (3.5 L) cake, top only	1 1/2 cups (375 mL)
13- by 9-inch (3.5 L) cake, top & sides	3 cups (750 mL)
2-layer (8-inch/20 cm) cake	2 3/4 to 3 cups (675 mL to 750 mL)
2-layer (9-inch/23 cm) cake	3 1/2 cups (875 mL)
8- or 9-inch (20 or 23 cm) square cake	2 to 2 1/2 cups (500 to 625 mL)
3- or 4-layer (8- or 9-inch/20 or 23 cm) cake	3 to 4 cups (750 mL to 1 L)
12 cupcakes	1 cup (250 mL)
Tube or Bundt cakes	3 1/2 cups (875 mL)

Cake size	Glaze required (approx)
13- by 9-inch (3.5 L) cake	1/2 to 1 cup (125 to 250 mL)
Tube or Bundt cakes	1 1/2 cups (375 mL)

CHUNKY CHOCOLATE PECAN COOKIES (PAGE 140) ➤

Basic Butter Frosting

Makes about 2 3/4 cups (675 mL) frosting; enough to fill and frost an 8-inch (20 cm) layer cake.

A versatile frosting that lends itself to a variety of flavors.

1/2 cup	butter, softened	125 mL
4 cups	confectioner's (icing) sugar, sifted	1 L
1/3 cup	light (10%) cream *or* evaporated milk	75 mL
1 tsp	vanilla extract	5 mL

1. In a large mixer bowl, cream butter and half of confectioner's sugar until light and creamy. Add cream and vanilla. Gradually add remaining confectioner's sugar, beating until smooth. Add a little more cream if frosting is too stiff, or a little more confectioner's sugar if too thin, to make a soft spreading consistency.

Lemon or Orange: Omit vanilla; add 1 tbsp (15 mL) lemon or orange juice and 1 tbsp (15 mL) grated lemon or orange zest.

Coffee: Blend 1 tbsp (15 mL) instant coffee powder into the butter.

Chocolate: Add 2 squares (each 1 oz [28 g]) unsweetened chocolate, melted and cooled, to creamed butter.

Cocoa: Replace 1/2 cup (125 mL) of the confectioner's sugar with 1/2 cup (125 mL) cocoa, sifted together with remaining confectioner's sugar.

Cherry: Decrease cream to 1/4 cup (50 mL). Omit vanilla. Add 1 tbsp (15 mL) maraschino cherry juice and fold in 1/2 cup (125 mL) well-drained, chopped cherries.

Cinnamon: Add 1/2 tsp (2 mL) ground cinnamon to creamed butter.

Berry: Omit cream and vanilla. Add 1/2 cup (125 mL) finely chopped or crushed fresh raspberries or strawberries.

◄ Caramel Pecan Bars (Page 152), Peanut Butter Chocolate Squares (Page 158)

Very Creamy Butter Frosting

Makes about 2 cups (500 mL) frosting; enough to frost a 9-inch (23 cm) square cake.

An extra creamy, buttery variation on a standard butter frosting.

TIP

Double the recipe to fill and frost a layer cake.

1/2 cup	butter, softened	125 mL
1 3/4 cups	confectioner's (icing) sugar, sifted	425 mL
1 tbsp	light (10%) cream	15 mL
1 tsp	vanilla extract	5 mL

1. In a small mixer bowl, beat butter until creamy. Gradually add confectioner's sugar alternately with cream, beating until smooth and creamy. Add vanilla and beat on high speed until light and fluffy.

Lemon or Orange: Omit vanilla. Add 1 tbsp (15 mL) lemon or orange juice and 1 tbsp (15 mL) grated lemon or orange zest.

Chocolate: Beat 2 squares (each 1 oz [28 g]) unsweetened chocolate, melted and cooled, into butter frosting.

Cooked Creamy Butter Frosting

Makes about 3 1/2 cups (825 mL) frosting; enough to fill and frost a 2-layer cake.

An old-fashioned frosting that has a rich, buttery, not-too-sweet taste. It has to be one of my favorites and well worth the extra cooking step.

1 cup	milk	250 mL
2 tbsp	all-purpose flour	25 mL
1 cup	butter, softened	250 mL
1 cup	granulated sugar	250 mL
1 tsp	vanilla extract	5 mL

1. In a small saucepan, whisk milk together with flour until smooth. Cook, stirring constantly, over medium heat until thickened. Remove from heat. Cover surface with plastic wrap. Cool thoroughly. In a large mixer bowl, cream butter, sugar and vanilla until light and fluffy. Gradually add thickened milk mixture, beating until light and creamy.

TIP

There's no substitute for real butter and real vanilla.

Banana Butter Frosting

Makes about 3 cups (750 mL) frosting; enough to fill and frost an 8-inch (20 cm) layer cake.

1/2 cup	butter, softened	125 mL
1/2 cup	mashed ripe bananas (1 or 2 bananas)	125 mL
4 cups	confectioner's (icing) sugar, sifted	1 L
1 tbsp	light (10%) cream	15 mL

1. In a large bowl, cream butter, mashed bananas and half of confectioner's sugar together on medium speed until light. Add cream. Add remaining confectioner's sugar gradually, beating until smooth and creamy.

Creamy Chocolate Butter Frosting

Makes about 1 1/2 cups (375 mL) frosting; enough to frost a 9-inch (23 cm) square cake.

A soft, light, creamy frosting made with stiffly beaten egg whites folded in.

TIP

Fold one-quarter of the stiff egg whites in thoroughly to soften mixture, then gently fold in remaining egg whites.

1/4 cup	butter, softened	50 mL
3/4 cup	confectioner's (icing) sugar, sifted	175 mL
1 tsp	vanilla extract	5 mL
3	squares (each 1 oz [28 g]) semi-sweet chocolate, melted and cooled	3
2	eggs whites	2

1. In a small mixer bowl, cream butter until smooth. Gradually add confectioner's sugar, beating until light and creamy. Blend in vanilla and chocolate, mixing well. Beat egg whites to stiff peaks. Fold into chocolate mixture gently but thoroughly.

Makes about 3 cups (750 mL) frosting; enough to fill and frost a 2-layer cake.

TIP

Gradually add a little more cream if frosting is too stiff or a little more confectioner's sugar if frosting is too soft.

Cocoa Butter Cream Frosting

3 cups	confectioner's (icing) sugar	750 mL
3/4 cup	cocoa	175 mL
2/3 cup	butter, softened	150 mL
5 to 6 tbsp	light (10%) cream or milk	75 to 90 mL
1 1/2 tsp	vanilla extract	7 mL

1. Sift confectioner's sugar and cocoa together; set aside. In a large mixer bowl, beat butter until smooth. Gradually add cocoa mixture alternately with cream, beating until smooth and creamy. (Add only enough cream to make a soft spreading consistency.) Beat in vanilla.

Very Peanut Buttery Frosting

Makes about 3 1/2 cups (875 mL) frosting; enough to fill and frost a 2-layer cake.

This frosting has a strong peanut butter flavor. It's nice on chocolate or peanut butter cake.

1 cup	creamy peanut butter	250 mL
1/2 cup	butter, softened	125 mL
2 cups	confectioner's (icing) sugar, sifted	500 mL
1/4 cup	milk	50 mL
1 tsp	vanilla extract	5 mL

1. In a large mixer bowl, beat peanut butter and butter on low speed until blended. Gradually add confectioner's sugar alternately with milk, mixing until thoroughly blended. Add vanilla. Beat on medium speed for 1 minute or until light and creamy.

TIP

Add finely chopped peanuts to frosting or sprinkle coarsely chopped peanuts on top to decorate cake.

Creamy Peanut Butter Frosting

Makes about 4 cups (1 L) frosting; enough to fill and frost a 2-layer cake.

This version is very creamy with a mild peanut butter flavor. It's good on chocolate and peanut butter cakes. A good choice for kids' cupcakes too.

3/4 cup	creamy peanut butter	175 mL
1/2 cup	butter, softened	125 mL
4 cups	confectioner's (icing) sugar, sifted	1 L
1/2 cup	milk	125 mL

1. In a large mixer bowl, beat peanut butter and butter until blended. Gradually add confectioner's sugar alternately with milk, beating on low speed until smooth. Beat on medium speed for 1 minute until light and creamy.

TIP

Decorate cake with chocolate-covered peanuts, halved peanut butter cups or chocolate peanut candy-coated pieces.

Chocolate Butter Frosting

Makes about 1 1/2 cups (375 mL) frosting; enough to frost a 9-inch (23 cm) square cake.

A soft, rich, velvety frosting made with the addition of egg yolks.

1/2 cup	butter, softened	125 mL
1 cup	confectioner's (icing) sugar, sifted	250 mL
2	egg yolks	2
3	squares (each 1 oz [28 g]) semi-sweet chocolate, melted and cooled	3

1. In a small mixer bowl, cream butter. Gradually add confectioner's sugar, beating until light and creamy. Add egg yolks, one at a time, beating thoroughly after each. Add melted chocolate, beating until smooth and creamy. Chill slightly, if necessary, to reach a soft spreading consistency.

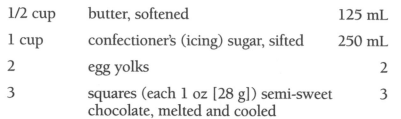

Lemon Butter Cream

Makes about 6 cups (1.5 L) frosting; enough to fill and frost a 4-layer cake.

Well worth every calorie. It makes a lot but some of it is bound to be eaten before it gets to the cake.

TIP

Use canned pie filling or cook a pudding and pie filling and cool before using.

1 1/2 cups	butter, softened	375 mL
3 cups	confectioner's (icing) sugar, sifted	750 mL
1 tbsp	lemon juice	15 mL
1	egg yolk	1
2 1/2 cups	prepared lemon pie filling	625 mL

1. In a large mixer bowl, cream butter until smooth. Gradually add half the confectioner's sugar. Beat in lemon juice, egg yolk and pie filling. Gradually add remaining confectioner's sugar, beating on medium speed until light and creamy. Chill if necessary to reach desired consistency.

Chocolate Rum Frosting

Makes about 2 cups (500 mL) frosting; enough to frost a 9-inch square cake or fill a 4-layer cake.

A wonderful, soft creamy filling and frosting with lots of flavor.

3/4 cup	butter, softened	175 mL
1 1/4 cups	confectioner's (icing) sugar, sifted	300 mL
2	egg yolks	2
1 tbsp	rum *or* 1 tsp (5 mL) rum extract	15 mL
6	squares (each 1 oz [28 g]) semi-sweet chocolate, melted and cooled	6

1. In a small mixer bowl, cream butter and confectioner's sugar until blended. Add egg yolks and rum, beating until smooth and creamy. Fold in melted chocolate gently but thoroughly. Chill slightly, if necessary, to reach spreading consistency.

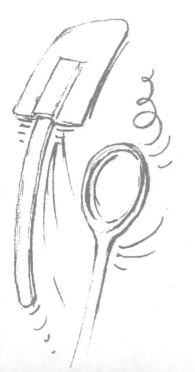

Light & Creamy Chocolate Frosting

Makes about 3 cups (750 mL) frosting; enough to frost a 9-inch (23 cm) layer cake.

A creamy milk chocolate flavor that looks striking with a drizzle of dark chocolate on top.

1/2 cup	butter, softened	125 mL
2	squares (each 1 oz [28 g]) unsweetened chocolate, melted and cooled	2
1/2 cup	confectioner's (icing) sugar, sifted	125 mL
1/2 cup	light (10%) cream	125 mL

1. In a large mixer bowl, cream butter and chocolate until blended. Add confectioner's sugar alternately with cream, beating until smooth. Beat on medium speed for 1 minute or until light and creamy. Add a little more confectioner's sugar if too soft or more cream if too stiff.

Makes about 2 1/2 cups (625 mL) frosting; enough to frost a 9-inch (23 cm) square cake.

A light, creamy chocolate color that looks and tastes terrific on dark chocolate cake.

Chocolate Sour Cream Frosting

1/4 cup	butter	50 mL
3	squares (each 1 oz [28 g]) semi-sweet chocolate, melted and cooled	3
1/2 cup	sour cream	125 mL
3 cups	confectioner's (icing) sugar, sifted	750 mL
2 tbsp	warm water	25 mL
1 tsp	vanilla extract	5 mL

1. In a small saucepan over low heat, combine butter and chocolate, stirring constantly until smoothly melted. Cool slightly. Transfer chocolate mixture to a large mixer bowl. Stir in sour cream. Gradually add confectioner's sugar alternately with warm water, beating on low speed until smooth and creamy. Beat in vanilla. Chill slightly, if necessary, to reach a soft spreading consistency

White Chocolate Coconut Hazelnut Frosting

Makes about 1 1/2 cups (375 mL) frosting; enough to frost an 8-inch (20 cm) square cake.

An elegant choice for white, spice or chocolate cakes.

VARIATION

Replace hazelnuts with pecans or almonds.

4	squares (each 1 oz [28 g]) white chocolate	4
1/4 cup	butter	50 mL
2 tbsp	light (10%) cream	25 mL
1/2 cup	flaked coconut	125 mL
1/2 cup	finely chopped hazelnuts	125 mL
1 cup	confectioner's (icing) sugar, sifted	250 mL

1. In a small saucepan, combine white chocolate, butter and cream. Heat, stirring constantly, over low heat until smooth. Cool 15 minutes. Add coconut, nuts and confectioner's sugar. Mix well. If necessary, add a little more confectioner's sugar or milk to reach a soft spreading consistency.

Basic Cream Cheese Frosting

Makes about 3 cups (750 mL) frosting; enough to fill and frost a 2-layer cake.

Don't limit this to carrot cake. It's very versatile. Try it on spice cake or chocolate cake.

8 oz	cream cheese, softened	250 g
1/2 cup	butter, softened	125 mL
1 tsp	vanilla extract	5 mL
3 to 3 1/2 cups	confectioner's (icing) sugar, sifted	750 to 825 mL

1. In a large mixer bowl, beat cream cheese, butter and vanilla on medium speed until fluffy. Gradually add confectioner's sugar, beating on medium speed until light and creamy. Add a little more confectioner's sugar if necessary to stiffen frosting.

   Orange: Omit vanilla. Add 2 tbsp (25 mL) orange juice and 1 tbsp (15 mL) grated orange zest to cheese mixture, alternately with confectioner's sugar.

   Pecan: Fold 1 cup (250 mL) finely chopped pecans into frosting.

   Pineapple: Omit vanilla. Increase confectioner's sugar to 4 cups (1 L). Fold in 1/3 cup (75 mL) well-drained crushed pineapple.

   Peach: Follow directions for Pineapple variation (above), but replace pineapple with 1/2 cup (125 mL) mashed and drained peaches.

   Berry: Follow directions for Pineapple variation (above), but replace pineapple with 1/2 cup (125 mL) mashed and drained fresh raspberries or strawberries.

White Chocolate Cream Cheese Frosting

Makes about 3 cups (750 mL) frosting; enough to frost a 2-layer cake.

A little sweet, but delicious. An unusual alternative to regular cream cheese frosting. Try it on chocolate cake – it's divine!

TIP

Use very low heat for melting white chocolate. It burns more easily than semi-sweet.

6 oz	white chocolate, chopped	180 g
8 oz	cream cheese, softened	250 g
1/4 cup	butter, softened	50 mL
3 cups	confectioner's (icing) sugar, sifted	750 mL

1. In a small saucepan over low heat, melt white chocolate, stirring constantly until smooth, or microwave on Medium 2 to 3 minutes until almost melted, then stir until smooth. Cool to room temperature. Beat cream cheese and butter in a large mixer bowl until blended. Add melted chocolate. Mix well. Gradually add confectioner's sugar, beating until smooth. Beat on medium speed for 1 minute or until light and creamy.

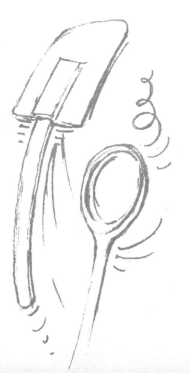

Chocolate Cream Cheese Frosting

Makes about 2 1/2 cups (625 mL) frosting; enough to frost a Bundt or tube cake.

6	squares (each 1 oz [28 g]) semi-sweet chocolate, chopped	6
1/4 cup	water	50 mL
8 oz	cream cheese, softened	250 g
2 cups	confectioner's (icing) sugar, sifted	500 mL

1. In a small saucepan over low heat, melt chocolate and water, or microwave on Medium in a large microwave-safe bowl for 2 to 3 minutes. Stir until chocolate is melted and smooth. Cool to lukewarm. In a large mixer bowl, beat cream cheese together with chocolate mixture on low speed until blended. Gradually add confectioner's sugar, beating until smooth.

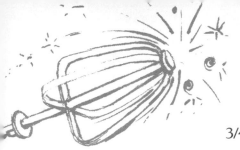

Quick Caramel Frosting

Makes about 4 cups (1 L) frosting; enough to frost a 13- by 9-inch (3.5 L) cake.

A soft, smooth caramel frosting that's lovely to spread on cakes. It's delicious on deep chocolate or banana cake. Similar to CARAMEL FROSTING (see recipe, page 174) but with a slightly milder caramel flavor.

3/4 cup	butter	175 mL
1 cup	packed brown sugar	250 mL
1/3 cup	evaporated milk *or* light (10%) cream	75 mL
3 cups	confectioner's (icing) sugar, sifted	750 mL
1 1/2 tsp	vanilla extract	7 mL

1. In a medium saucepan over low heat, combine butter and brown sugar, stirring until smooth. Blend in evaporated milk. Cool slightly. Gradually add confectioner's sugar and vanilla, beating to a soft spreading consistency.

Crunchy Broiled Topping

Makes about 2 1/2 cups (625 mL) topping; enough to top a 13- by 9-inch (3.5 L) cake.

TIP

Topping is spread on cake in the pan immediately or 5 minutes after it comes out of the oven.

Watch topping closely. It will burn quickly.

1/4 cup	butter	50 mL
3/4 cup	packed brown sugar	175 mL
1/4 cup	light (10%) cream	50 mL
1 cup	flaked coconut	250 mL
1 cup	chopped pecans	250 mL

1. In a saucepan melt butter. Stir in remaining ingredients. Preheat broiler. Spread topping evenly over hot cake. Broil 6 inches (15 cm) below element for about 3 minutes or until golden brown. Cool cake completely in pan on a wire rack before cutting.

Caramel Frosting

Makes about 3 cups (750 mL) frosting; enough to frost a 2-layer cake.

This icing is an excuse to bake a cake. I'm not sure whether I like it better on a cake or as a fudge!

TIP

Delicious on banana, spice, chocolate and carrot cake. In other words – almost any cake!

1/2 cup	butter	125 mL
1 cup	packed brown sugar	250 mL
1/4 cup	milk	50 mL
2 cups	confectioner's (icing) sugar, sifted	500 mL
3/4 tsp	vanilla extract	4 mL

1. In a medium saucepan, combine butter and brown sugar. Cook, stirring constantly, over medium heat until mixture comes to a boil. Add milk; bring mixture back to a boil. Remove from heat. Stir in confectioner's sugar and vanilla. Spread warm frosting immediately onto cake.

Flavored Whipped Creams

Makes about 2 cups (500 mL) whipped cream; enough to fill and frost a 9-inch (23 cm) layer cake.

This is the basic, slightly sweetened whipped cream from which you can make many different flavors.

TIP

Chill bowl, beaters and cream well before beating.

Double recipe as required.

VARIATION

Fold 1/4 cup (50 mL) crushed nut brittle, grated chocolate, chopped nuts, fruit or toasted coconut into stiffly whipped cream.

Basic Cream

1 cup	whipping (35%) cream	250 mL
2 tbsp	confectioner's (icing) sugar, sifted	25 mL

Flavor Variations

1 tsp	vanilla extract	5 mL
1/2 tsp	almond extract	2 mL
1/2 tsp	peppermint extract	2 mL
1/2 tsp	rum or brandy extract	2 mL
1/2 tsp	maple extract	2 mL
1/2 tsp	ground cinnamon	2 mL
1/2 tsp	ground nutmeg	2 mL
1/2 tsp	ground ginger	2 mL
1 1/2 tsp	grated lemon or orange zest	7 mL
1 1/2 tsp	instant coffee powder	7 mL

1. In a small mixer bowl, beat cream, confectioner's sugar and one of the flavorings together until stiff peaks form.

Apricot Whipped Cream Filling

Makes about 4 cups (1 L) filling; enough to fill and frost a 4-layer cake.

2 cups	whipping (35%) cream	500 mL
1/4 cup	confectioner's (icing) sugar, sifted	50 mL
1	jar (7 1/2 oz [213 mL]) apricot baby food	1

1. Beat whipping cream and confectioner's sugar to stiff peaks. Fold in apricot baby food, gently but thoroughly. Chill until using.

Chocolate Whipped Cream Filling & Frosting

Makes about 4 cups (1 L) frosting; enough to fill and frost top of a 4-layer cake.

TIP

Use plain or fold in 1 cup (250 mL) crushed chocolate toffee bars (Skor, Heath, Butterfinger).

2 cups	whipping (35%) cream	500 mL
1/2 cup	granulated sugar	125 mL
1/3 cup	cocoa, sifted	75 mL

1. In a small mixer bowl, combine cream, sugar and cocoa. Chill 15 minutes. Beat mixture to stiff peaks. Fold in crushed chocolate bars, if desired.

Pudding & Cream Filling & Frosting

Makes about 3 cups (750 mL) frosting; enough to fill and frost a 2-layer cake.

A simple cream frosting that can be adapted to any flavor of instant pudding.

1 cup	whipping (35%) cream	250 mL
1	pkg (4-serving size) instant pudding mix (banana, vanilla, pistachio, chocolate, lemon or butterscotch)	1
1 cup	milk	250 mL

1. In a small mixer bowl, beat cream to stiff peaks. Set aside. Beat pudding mix and milk on low speed for 1 minute. Let set 1 minute. Fold in whipped cream. Chill until using.

Jiffy Snow Frosting

Makes about 3 1/2 cups (825 mL) frosting; enough to fill a 2-layer cake or angel food cake.

An elegant fluffy white frosting that peaks like snow.

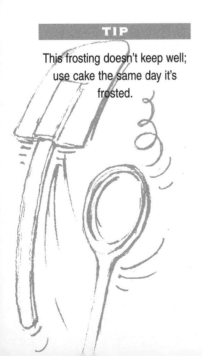

TIP

This frosting doesn't keep well; use cake the same day it's frosted.

1 1/4 cups	corn syrup	300 mL
2	egg whites	2
1 tsp	vanilla extract	5 mL
1/4 tsp	food coloring (optional)	1 mL

1. In a small saucepan, bring syrup to a boil. Beat egg whites in small mixer bowl to stiff but moist peaks. Gradually beat in hot syrup. Continue beating until very stiff and shiny, about 5 minutes. Beat in vanilla and coloring, if desired. Spread immediately on baked (cooled) cake.

Chocolate Ganache

Makes about 2 cups (500 mL) ganache; enough to frost a 9-inch (23 cm) square cake.

1 cup	whipping (35%) cream	250 mL
8 oz	semi-sweet chocolate, chopped	250 g
1 tbsp	liqueur (orange, coffee, raspberry, almond) (optional)	15 mL

One of the simplest but most amazing frostings for taste and appearance.

1. Place cream in a small saucepan. Bring to a boil, stirring often, over medium heat. Place chocolate in a large mixer bowl. Pour hot cream over chocolate, stirring until melted. Stir in liqueur, if desired. Let stand at room temperature until desired consistency is reached.

To Use

Glaze: Let ganache stand about 30 minutes. Pour evenly over top of cake, letting it drip down sides. Leave until chocolate sets.

Frosting: Let ganache stand 3 to 4 hours, or until a soft spreading consistency is reached. Spread over cake; leave to set.

TIP

You can use ganache for a glaze or a frosting. The only difference is the cooling time. The longer you leave it, the thicker it gets.

If ganache gets too firm, simply set over warm water, stirring to soften.

VARIATION

Replace semi-sweet with bittersweet chocolate.

Sweet & Sour Chocolate Frosting

Makes about 4 cups (1 L) frosting; enough to fill and frost a 3-layer cake.

The subtle blend of sweet and sour makes this a favorite frosting.

3 tbsp	butter, softened	45 mL
3	squares (each 1 oz [28 g]) semi-sweet chocolate, melted and cooled	3
4 1/2 cups	confectioner's (icing) sugar, sifted	1.13 L
3/4 cup	sour cream	175 mL
1 tsp	vanilla extract	5 mL

1. In a large mixer bowl, cream butter and chocolate until blended. Add confectioner's sugar and sour cream alternately, beating until smooth. Add vanilla. Beat on medium speed for 1 minute or until creamy.

Rocky Road Frosting

**Makes about 2 cups
(500 mL) frosting; enough
to fill and frost a
13- by 9-inch (3.5 L) cake
or 16 cupcakes.**

*Chockful of marshmallows,
nuts and chocolate –
almost like fudge.*

TIP

Spread frosting while warm.
It hardens quickly on cooling.

2	squares (each 1 oz [28 g]) unsweetened chocolate	2
1 cup	miniature marshmallows	250 mL
1/4 cup	butter	50 mL
1/4 cup	water	50 mL
2 cups	confectioner's (icing) sugar, sifted	500 mL
1 tsp	vanilla extract	5 mL
1 cup	miniature marshmallows	250 mL
1/2 cup	chopped pecans, walnuts or peanuts	125 mL

1. In a saucepan combine chocolate, 1 cup (250 mL) marshmallows, butter and water. Cook over low heat, stirring constantly until smoothly melted. Cool slightly. Transfer mixture to a large mixer bowl. Add confectioner's sugar and vanilla. Beat on medium speed for 2 minutes to obtain a soft, smooth spreading consistency. Stir in remaining marshmallows and nuts. Quickly spread over cake.

Basic Glazes

Glazes are a nice alternative to frosting. They give a simple finishing touch in taste and appearance. They are quick and easy to prepare too. They are usually drizzled warm over Bundt and tube cakes and will harden on cooling.

These are based on Basic Vanilla Glaze.

Orange or Lemon
Omit vanilla and water. Add 2 tsp (10 mL) grated orange or lemon zest and 2 to 4 tbsp (25 to 60 mL) orange or lemon juice.

Pineapple Orange
Omit vanilla and water. Add 1 tsp (5 mL) grated orange zest and 2 to 4 tbsp (25 to 60 mL) pineapple juice.

Coffee
Replace vanilla with 2 tsp (10 mL) instant coffee powder.

Vanilla or Almond

2 cups	confectioner's (icing) sugar, sifted	500 mL
1 tbsp	butter, softened	15 mL
1 tsp	vanilla or almond extract	5 mL
2 to 3 tbsp	hot water	25 to 45 mL

1. In a small bowl, combine confectioner's sugar and butter. Add flavoring and enough liquid to make a smooth pourable consistency.

Peanut Butter

2 cups	confectioner's (icing) sugar, sifted	500 mL
3 tbsp	creamy peanut butter	45 mL
3 to 5 tbsp	hot water	45 to 75 mL

Prepare as for Vanilla Glaze.

Brown Sugar Glaze

Makes about 3/4 cup (175 mL) glaze; enough to spread on top and drizzle down sides of Bundt or tube cake.

1/4 cup	packed brown sugar	50 mL
2 1/2 tbsp	light (10%) cream	37 mL
2 tbsp	butter	25 mL
2/3 cup	confectioner's (icing) sugar, sifted	150 mL

1. In a small saucepan over medium heat, combine brown sugar, cream and butter, stirring constantly until mixture comes to a boil. Remove from heat. Cool to room temperature. Add confectioner's sugar, beating until smooth. If necessary, add a little more confectioner's sugar or cream to make a drizzling consistency. Drizzle over cake.

Chocolate Glazes

There are many, many recipes for chocolate glaze, each a little different but all quite simple to make. They are warm to spread or drizzle and firm up on cooling. I've given you a few of my favorites here.

Basic Chocolate Glaze

1	square (1 oz [28 g]) unsweetened chocolate, chopped	1
1 tbsp	butter	15 mL
1/4 cup	water	50 mL
2 cups	confectioner's (icing) sugar, sifted	500 mL

1. In a small saucepan over low heat, melt chocolate, butter and water, stirring constantly until smooth. Remove from heat. Gradually add confectioner's sugar, stirring until smooth. Add a little more water, if necessary, to reach a pourable consistency.

Basic Chocolate Chip Glaze

1 cup	granulated sugar	250 mL
1/3 cup	butter	75 mL
1/3 cup	light (10%) cream	75 mL
1 cup	semi-sweet chocolate chips	250 mL
1/2 tsp	vanilla extract	2 mL

1. In a small saucepan, combine sugar, butter and cream. Cook over medium heat, stirring constantly, until mixture comes to a boil, then boil for 1 minute. Remove from heat. Add chocolate chips and vanilla, stirring until smoothly melted. Pour warm glaze over top of cake, letting it drizzle down sides.

VARIATION

Replace vanilla with 1/4 tsp (1 mL) almond extract and garnish cake with sliced almonds.

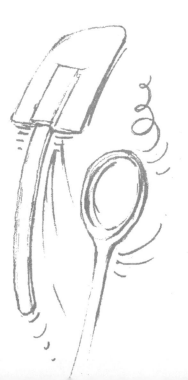

Chocolate Glazes continue...

Chocolate Glazes

(continued)

Chocolate Brandy Glaze

4	squares (each 1 oz [28 g]) semi-sweet chocolate, chopped	4
1/4 cup	butter	50 mL
2 tbsp	whipping (35%) cream	25 mL
1 tbsp	brandy or almond liqueur	15 mL

1. In a small saucepan over low heat, melt chocolate and butter, stirring constantly until smooth. Remove from heat. Add cream and brandy. Mix well. Pour over top of cake, letting it drip over sides.

Shiny Chocolate Mocha Glaze

4	squares (each 1 oz [28 g]) semi-sweet chocolate, chopped	4
2 tbsp	strong coffee	25 mL
3 tbsp	butter, softened	45 mL

1. In a small saucepan over low heat, melt chocolate and coffee, stirring constantly until smooth. Remove from heat. Gradually add butter, stirring until smooth. Pour over top of cake, letting it drip over sides.

Chocolate Peanut Butter Glaze

4	squares (each 1 oz [28 g]) semi-sweet chocolate, chopped	4
2/3 cup	creamy peanut butter	150 mL

1. In a small saucepan over low heat, melt chocolate and peanut butter, stirring constantly until smooth. Spread evenly over cake.

TIP

Replace brandy with 1 tsp (5 mL) almond extract.

TIP

A nice glaze to garnish with a sprinkling of chopped peanuts or crushed peanut brittle.

INDEX

Mousse filling, orange, 114-15
Muffins:
 apple oatmeal, 95
 blueberry, 96
 chocolate, 93
 cranberry banana, 94

N
Nuts, 11
 butterscotch squares, 145
 chocolate bars, 148
 topping, 17, 83
 See also specific nuts

O
Oats:
 apple muffins, 95
 chocolate macadamia nut cookies, 134
 chocolate raspberry almond bars, 143
 peach cobbler, 117
Orange(s):
 angel food cream cake, 60
 buttercream, 40-41
 butter cream frosting, 165
 butter frosting, 161
 chiffon cake, 64
 chocolate jubilee cake, 40-41
 cream, 60
 cream cheese frosting, 170
 delight, 111
 glaze, 64, 65, 181
 mandarin,
  cake, 38
  soufflé cake, 114-15
  to buy, 38
 soufflé cake, 114-15

P
Peach(es):
 almond angel roll, 98
 and blueberry pudding cake, 68
 cake, 23
 cobbler, 117
 and cream cake, 52
 cream cheese frosting, 170
 filling, 117
 meringue shortcake, 44-45
Peach fruit pie filling, peach cake, 23
Peach gelatin mix, peaches 'n' cream cake, 52
Peanut butter:
 chocolate and banana cake, 16

Peanut butter (continued):
 chocolate glaze, 16
 cookies, 138
 frosting, 165
Peanut butter chips, chocolate squares, 158
Pecans:
 and apricot glaze, 48
 blueberry coffee cake, 85
 butterscotch nut bars, 157
 caramel bars, 152
 and chocolate chip topping, 32
 chocolate cookies, 140
 cranberry bars, 155
 cream cheese frosting, 170
 and marshmallow topping, 22
 pumpkin pie crunch, 99
 to toast, 22
Piña colada cake, 62
Pineapple:
 banana cake, 70
 butter frosting, 70
 carrot cake, 35
 chocolate carrot cake, 67
 coconut topping, 30
 cream cheese frosting, 78, 170
 Hawaiian dream cake, 78
 lemon cake, 120
 mandarin cake, 38
 orange glaze, 181
 piña colada cake, 62
 upside-down cake, 26
Pistachio nuts, lemon cake, 73
Poppy seeds:
 lemon layer cake, 50-51
 to store, 50
Praline cake, 20
Pumpkin:
 cake, 105
 cheesecake, 127
 cupcakes, 108
 pie crunch, 99

Q
Quick caramel frosting, 173

R
Rainbow dessert cake, 28
Raisins:
 carrot cake with, 24
 to plump, 24